Cross Stitcher
MAGAZINE'S

Complete Introduction to
Cross Stitch

Wendy Gardiner

First published in 1995 by
Future Books
A division of Future Publishing Limited
30 Monmouth Street, Bath BA1 2BW

Designed by Maria Bowers
Text by Wendy Gardiner
Edited by Kate John
Photographic styling by Lez Gardiner
Photography by Graham Cooper and Lez Gardiner

A CIP catalogue record of this book is
available from the British Library

ISBN: 1 85981 002 0

Printed and bound in Malaysia
by Times Offset (M) SDN BHD Group

2 4 6 8 10 9 7 5 3 1

We take great care to ensure that what we print is accurate, but
we cannot accept liability for any mistakes or misprints.

If you would like more information on our other stitching titles
please write to: The Publisher, Future Books at the above address

CONTENTS

CHAPTER ONE
THE BASICS

Getting Started 6

Alphabet 10

Pencil Case 12

Bookmarks 14

Cake Frills 16

Sampler 18

CHAPTER TWO . . . .
HOME DECORATING IDEAS

Towel Treatment 22

Frame Favourites 24

Fuchsia Inspired Lampshade 26

Decorative Cushion 28

Pillowslip Edging 30

Butterfly Napkin Set 32

Matching Table Cloth 34

CHAPTER THREE
WITH CHILDREN IN MIND

Advent Calendar 38

Pinafore Bib 40

Dungaree Bib 42

Hairband and Braces 44

Birthday Picture 46

CHAPTER FOUR
FOR THE KITCHEN

Jar Lacies 50

Cafe Style Curtains 52

Napkin Rings 54

Matching Napkin 56

Pot Holder 58

Kitchen Roller Blind 60

Teatime Tray Cloth 62

Timely Tea Cosy 64

CHAPTER FIVE
GIFTS

Gift Tags 68

Keep in Touch Writing Case 70

Spectacles Case 72

CHAPTER SIX
PERSONALISED CARDS

Happy Birthday 74

Christmas Designs 76

Special Occasions 78

KEY TO PROJECTS

TIME		DIFFICULTY	
🕐🕐🕐	Less than a month.	🧵🧵🧵	Skilled
🕐🕐	Less than a week.	🧵🧵	Intermediate
🕐	An evening.	🧵	Beginner

FOREWORD

Cross Stitcher magazine's *Complete Introduction to Cross Stitch* has over 30 inspiring new ideas for the home, all beautifully photographed in full colour. The easy to follow step-by-step photography and clear charts make every project easily approachable, even for absolute beginners.

Choose from practical gifts that are easy to make, beautifully co-ordinated sets for kitchen or bedroom or commemorative designs to keep forever.

The informative 'Basics' section, accompanied by colourful photographs, explains essential information on materials and techniques to ensure perfect results every time.

chapter 1
THE BASICS

GETTING STARTED

SIMPLE CROSS STITCH

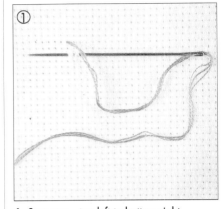

1. Step one – top left to bottom right.

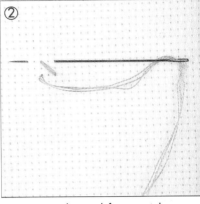

2. Step two – bottom left to top right.

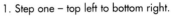

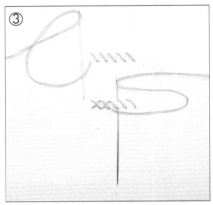

3. Work in rows in two stages. First, form lower cross then work back along the row to complete the upper cross.

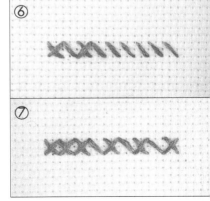

4. Work in rows in four stages. Firstly, work every other lower cross.

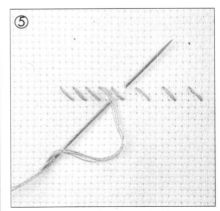

5. Second stage, fill in the missed lower cross on the same row.

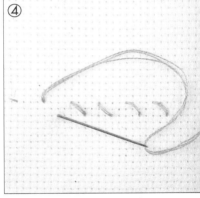

6. Thirdly, work along the row forming alternative top crosses.

7. Finally, form the remaining top crosses.

STITCHES

A cross stitch is simply one that is formed by two or more stitches crossing each other. The angle of the cross decides the type of cross stitch, which varies from a simple straight cross to, say, the more complicated interlaced Maltese Cross.

It is important to note that the top diagonal cross should always be worked in the same direction – unless an obvious light-shade effect is desired. Simple cross stitch can be worked in three basic ways.

When using canvas it is best to stitch each complete cross individually before proceeding to the next one. It is also essential that each cross stitch completely covers the canvas, so the thread choice is important.

The second method of working a cross stitch is to work a row. This is particularly suited to plain or evenweave fabric such as gingham. Simply work a line of diagonal stitches in one direction and then work back along the line in the opposite direction.

The third option, only suitable for evenweave fabrics, is a variation on the row method and is particularly useful when working a large design area. The lower row of diagonals is worked in two journeys and then the top row of diagonals is worked again in two journeys, each stitch completed alternately.

Other stitches used in conjunction with cross stitch for outlining or embroidery include:

Basting/Tacking Stitch

Used to mark the design area of holed fabrics together before sewing. The stitches are then removed once the design is complete. Use bold contrasting colour of thread so that it is easy to see.

Slip Stitch

To give an almost invisible finish on hems, facings etc. Use thread that matches the fabric for best results. Catch a strand or two of fabric, slide approximately 0.4cm along and up through the folded hem or facing. Catch another strand or two of main fabric, directly below and repeat to the end.

Running Stitch

Stitch in one direction along a complete line, leaving gaps between stitches. Return along the line, filling in the gaps to create an unbroken line using just one strand of thread.

Backstitch

Stitch each straight stitch individually when outlining a shape. Again, use only one strand of thread so that the outline does not dominate the design.

FABRICS

There are three main fabric categories for cross stitch designs; evenweave, plain weave and canvas.

Canvas

Canvas is made of vertical and horizontal threads woven together to produce precisely spaced holes between threads, resulting in a regular grid-like structure.

Canvas can be made from stiffened cotton, linen, silk gauze or plastic. It is commonly available in white or ecru. The two main types of canvas are single canvas and double canvas. The single version is formed by single vertical and horizontal threads whilst the double canvas, logically, has pairs of vertical and horizontal threads.

Canvas comes in a wide range of gauges (count). The count is the number of threads which can be stitched in 2.5cm (1in); for example, 11 HPI = holes per inch. Coarser count, say 3HPI – 5HPI is suitable for rugs.

Evenweave Fabric

Evenweave fabrics are particularly suited to basic Cross Stitch. They are, as the name suggests, made up by an equal quantity and thickness of vertical and horizontal threads, providing the same number of threads in a given area. Most popular evenweave fabrics are *Aida*, *Hardanger*, *Ainring* and *Glenshee*.

Aida has four threads woven together to form distinct blocks over which the stitches are formed, whilst *Hardangar* fabric has pairs of threads woven together.

The size of the stitches can be easily varied with evenweave fabric simply by working each stitch over more or less threads of the weave. For instance, a stitch worked over five threads of the evenweave will obviously be larger than one worked over three threads.

Plain Weave Fabrics

Plain weave fabrics can be difficult to use and only those with a regular woven or printed design, such as gingham, can be easily used for Cross Stitch. With these, the pattern in the fabric provides the necessary grid for working crossed stitches evenly and neatly and facilitates following a graph. Pitfalls to avoid are choosing too fine a fabric for the thread, which

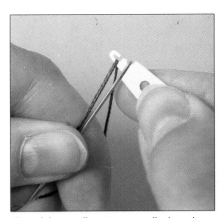

Thread the needle using a needle threader.

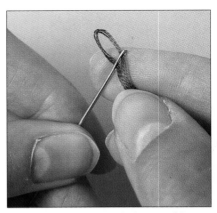

Slip the crisp loop through the eye of the needle.

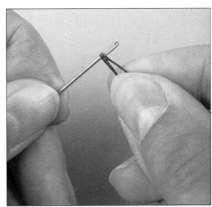

Thread the needle manually – loop the thread around the needle eye, pull firmly.

will result in a distorted or puckered background. It is also best to choose a fabric that is firmly woven and will allow the thread to be passed easily in and out.

THREADS

Embroidery threads come in a wide range of colours and weights. Some skeins of thread are multi-stranded and can be divided to create the thickness/weight

Suitable fabrics for cross stitching.

> **TIP**
> If you choose to use a different count canvas to that called for, remember that the finished piece will be a different size. A finer count (more stitches per inch) will produce a smaller piece whilst a coarser gauge will produce a larger piece.

required; others are twisted and must be used as one thread.

In this book, we have mostly used stranded thread. This is a loosely twisted thread, usually made up of six strands that is slightly shiny. The skeins can be separated into single strands and worked in any combination from one to six strands, depending on the project. Although the colour range is extremely extensive, it can be easily extended to create individual colours by mixing strands from different skeins.

Other threads that are suited to cross stitch include:
Pearl Cotton – a twisted 2-ply thread with high sheen that is used as supplied. **Soft Embroidery Cotton** – a 5-ply thread which is fairly thick and has a matt finish. Generally it is used as a single thread on heavier fabrics.
Stranded Pure Silk – a 7-ply, shiny thread that can be divided. Whilst many brilliant colours are available, silk is more difficult than cotton to work with and does need

to be dry-cleaned. **Tapestry Wool** – a tightly twisted 4-ply wool – used on coarse canvas for rugs etc.

FRAMES

There are two basic types of frame; ring and roller frames. Frames are used to keep the fabric taut whilst working on the design, which will prevent distortion and puckering, as well as help keep stitches even.

The ring frames, available in a variety of sizes are made from two rings. The fabric is laid between the two, which are then tightened by a screw holding the fabric firmly

Divide stranded cotton and use two or three threads at a time.

in place.

However, if marks are left by the ring, they can be difficult to remove. Therefore, it is advisable to ensure that the completed design is well within the frame. To avoid marks, bind the inner ring with tissue or fabric.

The roller frame is used primarily for large pieces of work. The fabric or canvas is tacked to the top and bottom rollers and then laced to the sides to hold taut.

OTHER EQUIPMENT

Whilst it is not essential to have other specific equipment to complete any cross stitch design, there are many items available that are a great help. The usual sewing accessories such as, a fine pair of embroidery scissors; tape measure, sharp glass-headed pins; choice of needles; pin cushion and sewing machine can be complemented by other specialist aids, designed to simplify work and make it more enjoyable.

These aids include such items as a *Needle Threader*, particularly one that copes with thicker thread; *Project Cards* to hold threads for

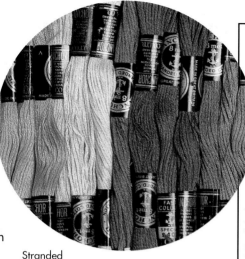

Stranded cotton.

easy identification and *Needleholder Cards* with magnetic strips to hold threaded needles – particularly useful for designs with many colour changes. *Magnetic Boards* with magnetic strips will hold graphs in place whilst a *Line Magnifier* will help amplify small or complex graphs. Alternatively a magnifier that hangs from the neck and props against the body is a great way to keep both hands free for handling the work, whilst enlarging the area to be worked on. Finally, a *Project Carrying Case*, with ample pockets for threads, haberdashery and projects will keep everything together.

USEFUL TIPS

1 **Thread** – use thread in lengths of approximately 40cm (15¾in) to avoid tangling. Longer threads also have a tendency to fray and can lose their natural sheen if over handled.

2 **Starting and Finishing** – avoid using knots as these may well show through or cause a lump. Instead use 2-3 tiny back stitches in a space that will later be covered by stitches.
Alternatively, leave a tail (approximately 5cm/2in)) which can be darned in later. When finishing, slide the needle through a row of stitches, approximately 3cm (1¼in) long, before cutting off the loose end.

3 **Frames** – bind the inner round frames in a length of cotton tape to help prevent marking and/or damage to fabric. Secure with masking tape.

4 **Fabric** – prevent edges fraying whilst working by running a line of machine stitching around the edges. Also allow at least 12cm (5in) extra for work that will be framed and 7cm (3in) for all unframed pieces.

5 **Transferring Designs to Fabric** – when working from a chart on evenweave fabric or canvas, simply follow the chart by counting the threads to determine where to position the stitch. With plain weave fabrics you might prefer to trace the design onto the fabric or tack it in place.

6 **Basting/Tacking** – it is advisable to plot with tacking stitches the area to be worked – the centre, borders, and corners etc.

A selection of sewing aids.

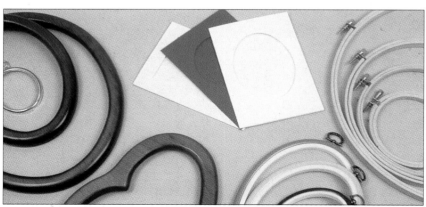

Frames and mounts for cross stitch designs.

ALPHABET

STITCHING INSTRUCTIONS

The very nature of cross stitch epitomises handcrafted gifts and treasured mementoes. It is therefore a good idea when starting cross stitch to practice simple numbers and an alphabet. We have chosen an evenweave 11HPI pearl aida and DMC stranded cotton. The 11HPI aida is ideal for medium size cross stitch and simple designs whilst the six strand thread can be divided into single strands to suit the needs of the various projects. Generally, three strands of stranded cotton will produce an even, fully covered area.

These will always be useful for a variety of projects, and can later be incorporated into many other personalised designs.

STITCHING THE ALPHABET

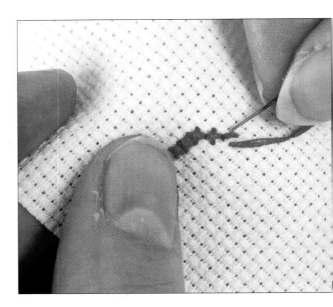

1 Starting from the back, secure the thread and then pull the needle through to the front. Sew each cross stitch individually, starting each stitch at the same point each time – ie: bottom left over to top right, under to bottom right, over to top left, under to bottom left of next etc.

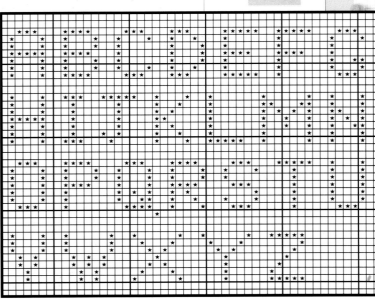

3 When planning the motto or text for a personalised memento, remember to bear in mind the varying heights and width of each letter/number used. Calculate the number of holes each requires, plus spaces between letters and words. The simplest method is to write on a piece of graph paper, using each square as a stitch with each of the intersections of the ruled lines as one hole.

2 Each letter or number is counted over a specific number of holes. For instance, when using lower case letters remember that some will have ascenders and descenders that will need to be higher or deeper than those without, so extra space between rows of text are necessary. Equally, letters that are wider, such as M or W will take up more space horizontally than others.

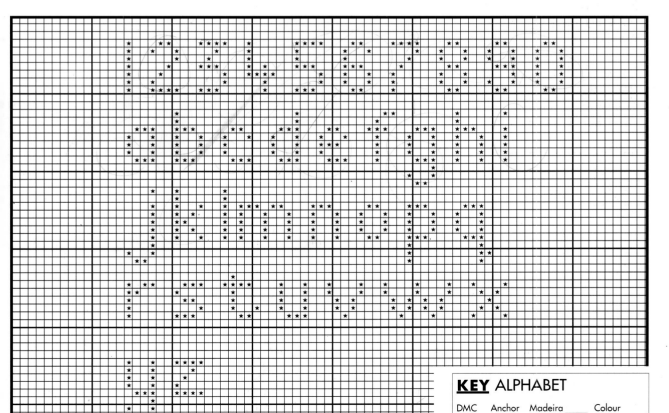

KEY ALPHABET				
DMC	Anchor	Madeira		Colour
817	47	0510	■ ■	RED
721	316	0309	★ ★	ORANGE

PENCIL CASE

Create this brightly coloured, personalised accessory for children, to fill with their favourite pencils and pens.

STITCHING INSTRUCTIONS

KEY PENCIL CASE

DMC	Anchor	Madeira		Colour
820	139	0904	⊙ ⊙	BLUE
543	372	2013	● ●	CREAM

MAKING THE PENCIL CASE

1 Using a nice bright red 14HPI aida, cut a piece approximately 23 x 26cm (9 x 10in). Mark the area in which the lettering is to go – the top line approximately 6cm from top fabric edge. Allow at least 9 clear holes between lines of lettering. Then, start lettering, approximately 4cm from the left edge, using three strands of embroidery thread.

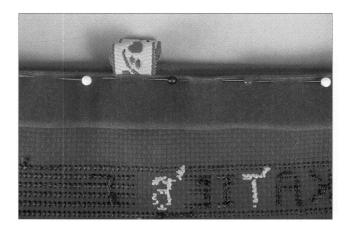

4 Turn raw edges in approximately 20cm (7in) at top and bottom. Cut velcro to fit along these edges, which will form the opening, and pin in place. At the same time, add small ribbon loops sandwiched between raw edge and velcro back. Baste and then machine stitch velcro to turned edge along the outer edge, ensuring you catch the ribbon loops as you go.

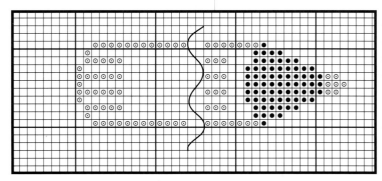

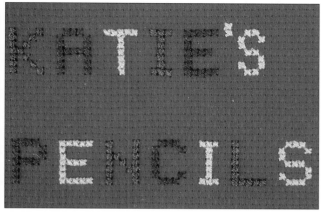

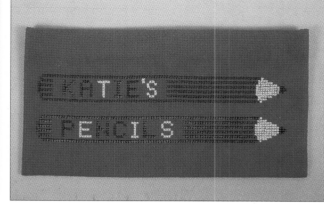

2 Leave one clear hole between each letter and change the colour of thread for each different letter if desired. Work each stitch separately, until the first line is complete. Then add the second row of wording within the tacked lines and leaving 9 clear holes between rows.

3 Following the chart, cross stitch the pencils around the two rows of wording, using three strands of thread. The pencil end should start approximately 2cm from the left edge, finishing with the pencil tip approximately 2.5cm (1in) from right edge. Fold the aida in half lengthways to check the design is nicely centred before turning, right sides together, ready to sew.

5 Fold the aida in half, with right sides together, and top velcro edges matching. Then machine stitch approximately 1cm from the selvage. Overlook the stitched seams to secure firmly and prevent fraying. Turn to right side and press, using a dry press cloth and warm iron.

BOOK MARKS

A stylish addition to any good book.

STITCHING INSTRUCTIONS

KEY BOOK MARKS

DMC	Anchor	Madeira		Colour
957	50	0613	● ●	PINK
326	47	0509	× ×	RED

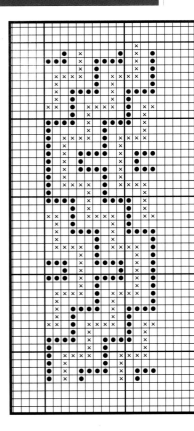

MAKING THE BOOKMARKS

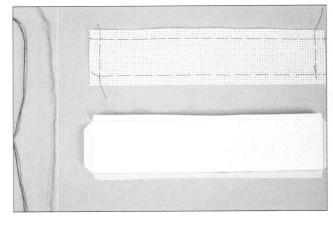

1 Prepare the book mark mount from card or heavy weight paper, cutting a piece approximately 5cm wide x 18cm (2 x 7in) in length. Score border approximately 0.7cm wide around the edge, trimming the four corners off so that when folded over, they will mitre neatly. Using 14 HPI fabric, cut a piece approximately 7 x 21cm (2¾ x 8¼in). Tack stitch around the outer edge of the design area.

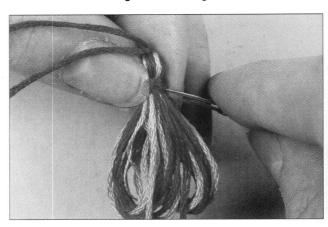

4 To make a co-ordinating tassel, simply wrap full strands of both colours around two fingers about six times. Holding one end firmly between thumb and fingers, stitch through the other end and then wrap the thread around the neck of the tassel until it is firmly bound together. Leave two long ends to secure the bookmark. Cut through the loops at the loose end, separating the strands with a pin to fan out.

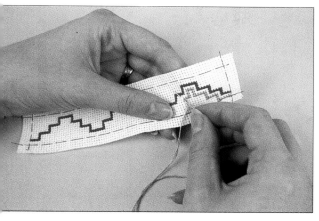

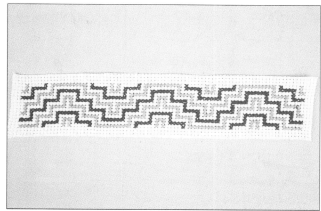

2 Start the design in the main colour, following the chart. When the centre of the design is reached, simply reverse the pattern to complete the other half of the design. Next, using the second colour, work another row of the design. Any design can be used from names to pictures although simple geometric designs are easier to follow.

3 Fill in the remainder of the design area, using three strands of stranded cotton and working each colour alternatively until complete. A third colour could be added to completely cover the background if desired. Remove the tacking stitch border and then trim the finished piece to approximately 3.5 x 16.5cm (1 3/8 x 6 1/2 in).

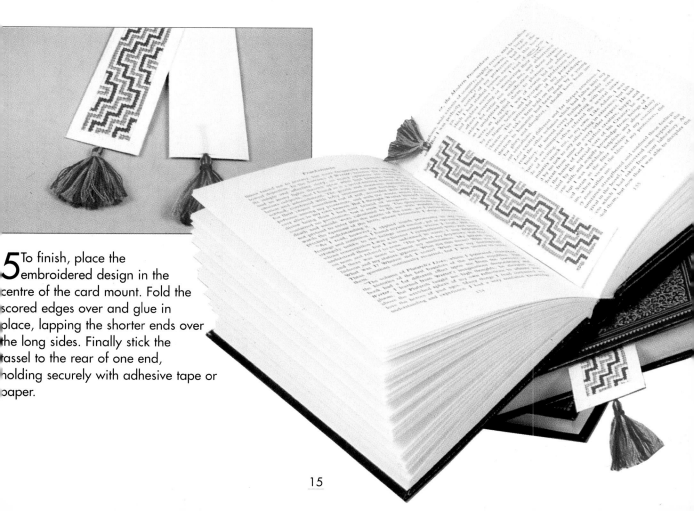

5 To finish, place the embroidered design in the centre of the card mount. Fold the scored edges over and glue in place, lapping the shorter ends over the long sides. Finally stick the tassel to the rear of one end, holding securely with adhesive tape or paper.

CAKE FRILLS

Impress your family and friends with this festive stitching.

STITCHING INSTRUCTIONS

KEY CAKE FRILLS

DMC	Anchor	Madeira			Colour
817	19	0211	#	#	RED
890	879	1314	●	●	GREEN
743	302	018	ƨ	ƨ	YELLOW

MAKING THE CAKE FRILLS

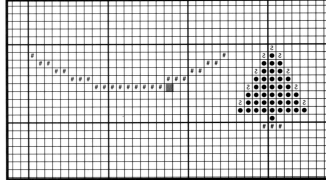

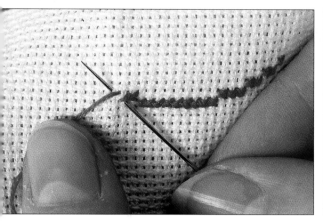

1 Cut a piece of 5cm wide 16HPI trim to fit snugly around your Christmas cake adding 4cm for seam allowances. (If cake size is not known, err on the generous side as any excess can always be overlapped.) Working with two strands of bright red embroidery thread and following the chart, begin the first garland 8 holes from top edge.

2 Leave 9 holes between garlands for the Christmas Tree. Again, following chart, cross stitch the tree using two strands of deep green embroidery thread. Finish each tree with a bright red base to match the garlands. Then add a row of candles using just one strand of thread. Work a cross stitch candle to alternate rows on either side of the tree and all three top rows.

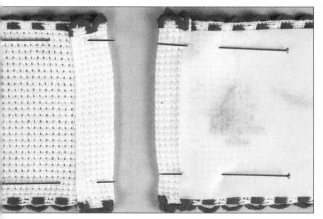

3 On the underside of the cake frill, turn in the ends once approximately 1cm and then again to encase the raw edges. Pin in place. Cut a piece of greaseproof paper to the finished length to fit within the trim edges, say 4.5cm (1 3/4 in) wide. Attach a cake frill with tiny stitches at intervals to hold in place.

4 Once the cake icing is set, add the embroidered cake frill, joining the ends at the back of the cake. If necessary, overlap the frill to fit snugly around the cake. Pin in place, preferably with glass headed pins that are easy to remove.

SAMPLER

Stitch this delightfully traditional sampler to celebrate a special occasion, or to be enjoyed as a lasting memento.

STITCHING INSTRUCTIONS

KEY SAMPLER

DMC	Anchor	Madeira			Colour
814	70	0601	●	●	BURGUNDY
605	74	0607	J	J	PINK
414	273	1801	×	×	GREY
605	74	0607	☐	☐	PINK
18 & ROSETTE					
414	273	1801	×	×	GREY
605	74	0607	J	J	PINK
814	70	0601	●	●	BURGUNDY
KEYS & BORDER					
605	74	0607	J	J	PINK
814	70	0601	●	●	BURGUNDY

MAKING THE SAMPLER

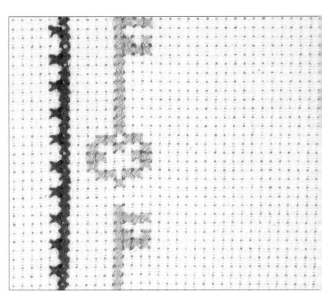

1 Cut the 11HPI pearl aida to approximately 40cm (15 ¾ in) square and mark the outer edge of the design area with a tacking stitch. Begin the border design seven holes from the edge, following the chart. Work around the whole edge using 3 strands of burgundy thread for the border. Leave one clear hole between border and key motif and then complete the line of keys using pale pink cotton.

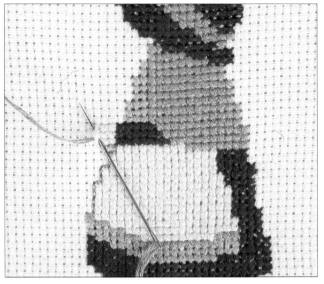

2 Once the design and motto has been completed, back stitch an outline around the edge of the little girl's pinafore and hand, using a single strand of the role pink thread. In this project, an 18th birthday has been highlighted in silver to contrast with the pinks. Use the alphabet and numerical charts on page 10 to personalise your own design.

3 Once the sampler is completed, cut a piece of card approximately 25.5cm (10in) square. Centre the design carefully over the card, folding the excess fabric to the back (approximately 5cm/2in all around – trim any excess away). Hold in place temporarily with dabs of tape and then lace the back over the card, using strong mercerised cotton. Pull the aida taut to hold securely in place and then fasten off.

4 Slip the finished sampler into a suitable frame, staining the wood to match if preferred. Add another piece of card as backing, cutting the size to fit snugly in the frame. Hold in place with heavy duty tape. Finally, add a hanging hook to the back, again using heavy duty tape to secure firmly.

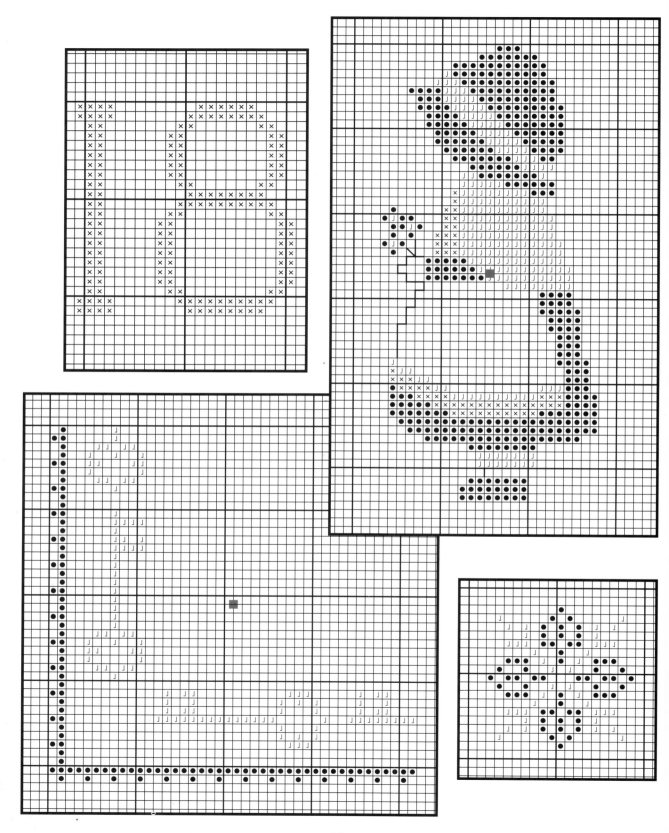

chapter 2
HOME
DECORATING
IDEAS

TOWEL TREATMENT

This flower design will add an appliquéd flair to your towels.

STITCHING INSTRUCTIONS

KEY TOWEL

DMC	Anchor	Madeira		Colour
437	368	2011	× ×	BEIGE
327	100	0714	◖ ◖	VIOLET
701	227	1305	♥ ♥	GREEN
743	302	0108	● ●	YELLOW
219	108	0802	⊙ ⊙	MAUVE

MAKING UP THE TOWEL

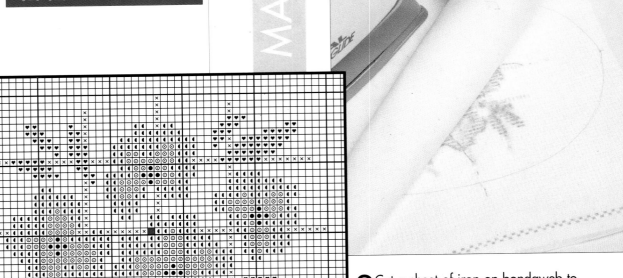

3 Cut a sheet of iron-on bondaweb to approximately 23cm (9in) square. Draw a large oval on the paper backing, that will nicely frame the cross stitch pattern. Place this over the wrong side of the finished design and iron on, using a dry press cloth and fairly hot iron.

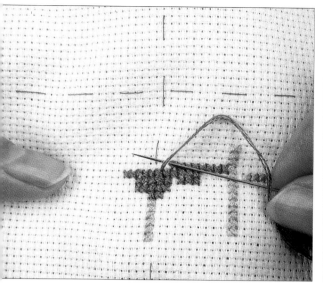

1 Cut a 23cm (9in) square of 14HPI aida and tack the edges to prevent them from fraying. Mark the centre, using two rows of long running stitches. Begin the design at a convenient point, working each stitch individually using DMC cotton perle and following the chart.

2 Continue working the design, following the chart. When changing colour, avoid trailing threads across the back of the work as they may show through, instead, tie off each flower or trellis and start again.

4 Holding the stiffened design in one hand, cut out around the oval shape. The bondaweb will prevent the aida edges from fraying. Place the oval onto a towel at the centre of one end.

5 Secure the oval in place using a warm iron and dry press cloth. Press firmly to make the bondaweb adhesive stick. Finally, machine stitch the oval edges to the towel, using a tight zigzag or overlocking stitch.

FRAME FAVOURITES

Dress up a frame for a favourite portrait.

STITCHING INSTRUCTIONS

KEY FRAME

DMC	Anchor	Madeira			Colour
3818	218	1405	●	●	DARK GREEN
471	265	1603	◖	◖	PALE GREEN
718	88	0706	♥	♥	DARK PINK
604	51	0614	·	·	PALE PINK

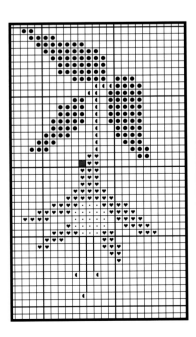

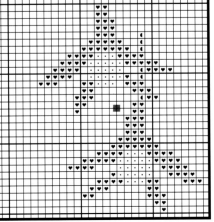

MAKING THE FRAME

3 Cut a piece of cotton poplin to line the frame – it should be just within the frame dimensions. Machine stitch to right side of aida along the picture (inner) edge running stitch, pivoting at the corners. Remove the tacking stitches and trim centre piece approximately 0.5cm from the stitching.

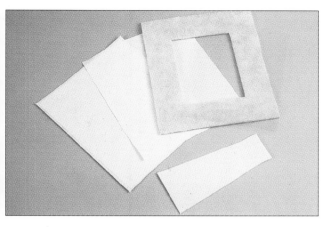

1 Prepare the picture frame components – using mounting card for the backing, strut and frame front. Cut the back and front pieces approximately 19 x 22cm (7½ x 8¾in). Cut out the picture area, approximately 10.5 x 13.5cm (4⅛ x 5¼ in) and glue some wadding to the front piece to provide padding. Cover the back with cotton poplin.

2 Cut a piece of 11HPI aida approximately 24 x 29cm (9¼ x 11½ in). Mark the front frame section and picture area, approximately 10.5 x 13.5cm (4⅛ x 5¼ in) with running stitches. Following the chart, cross stitch two overlapping fuchsia in one corner and a group of leaves in the opposite corner, using DMC cotton perle.

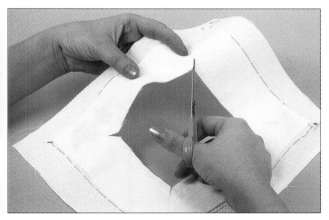

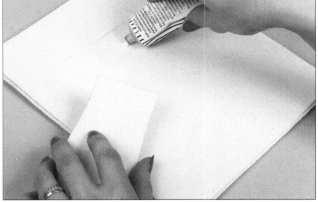

4 Once the centre pieces have been trimmed away, clip the corners diagonally to within 1mm of stitching. Turn the lining to wrong side, folding along the stitching line. Pin and press to form a crisp edge. Insert the padded card, prepared earlier. Fold the outer edges of aida over the card, lap with the lining and glue in place.

5 Glue the covered back to front at three sides, leaving the top open to insert photograph. Score across the strut approximately 2.5cm (1in) from narrow end and then cover the strut with cotton poplin. With double-sided tape or glue, stick the strut to the back of the frame, ensuring the bottom of frame and strut are equal.

FUCHSIA INSPIRED LAMPSHADE

Brighten up your lampshade with this colourful fuchsia design.

STITCHING INSTRUCTIONS

MAKING THE LAMPSHADE

KEY LAMPSHADE

DMC	Anchor	Madeira		Colour
3818	218	1405	● ●	DARK GREEN
471	265	1603	◐ ◐	PALE GREEN
718	88	0706	♥ ♥	DARK PINK
604	51	0614	· ·	PALE PINK

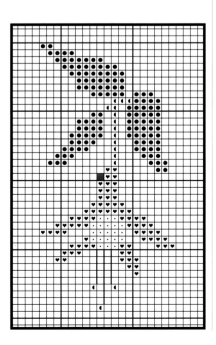

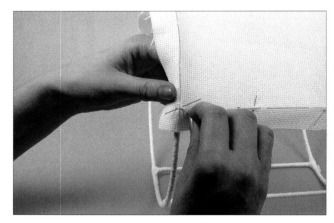

3 Pin the aida to the taped frame along the running stitches. Hand stitch to the frame, folding in the 1cm seam allowance of the aida at the top and bottom of the frame. Overlap the two side edges, turning the raw edge of the top piece under and then hand stitch to the frame through both edges.

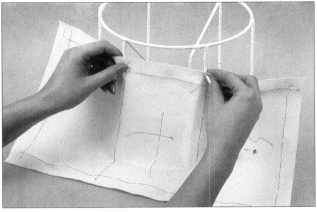

1 Using cotton bias binding, bind your chosen lampshade frame, wrapping the tape around each part very tightly. Secure with one or two stitches where each vertical pole meets the top and bottom of the frame.

2 Cut two pieces of 11HPI aida approximately 2cm deeper and wider than half of the frame. Using contrasting thread and large running stitches, mark the frame dimensions and panels on the aida. In addition, mark the centre of each panel. Cross stitch a single fuchsia in each panel, following the chart.

4 Add the braid along the top edge of the frame, either by gluing in place or by hand stitching. Also cover the side seams with a line of braid, again either glued or stitched in place.

5 Glue the fringing around the bottom edge of the lampshade, so that the fringing hangs down. Finally, add the braid trim over the fringing to match the top and side braiding. Again glue or stitch in place.

DECORATIVE CUSHION

A delightful cushion, the design of which is both delicate and stylish in detail.

STITCHING INSTRUCTIONS

KEY CUSHION

DMC	Anchor	Madeira		Colour
3818	218	1405	● ●	DARK GREEN
471	265	1603	◖ ◖	PALE GREEN
718	88	0706	♥ ♥	DARK PINK
604	51	0614	· ·	PALE PINK

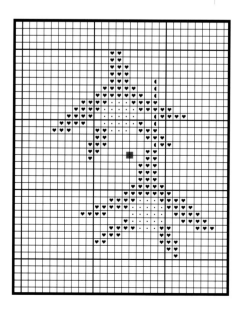

MAKING THE CUSHION

1 Cut a small piece of 11HPI aida approximately 16cm (6¼in) square. Mark the centre using a contrasting thread and two lines of long running stitches. Following the chart and using DMC cotton perle, cross stitch the overlapping fuchsias.

4 To make the cushion cover, simply cut two fabric squares approximately 2cm larger than the cushion. Add the lace trimmed panel to the centre of one cover piece, either using bondaweb or machine stitching around the edges. Sandwich *embroidery anglais* edging between right sides of cover and stitch three sides of the cushion. Turn and press. Insert cushion, slip stitch remaining edge and trim together.

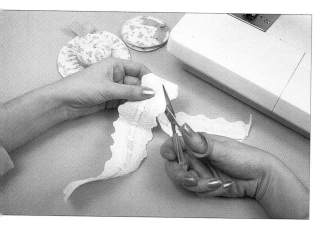

2 Cut two lengths of ribbon threaded lace trim approximately 32cm (12½in) long – to fit around the cross stitch panel. Prepare the corners by folding lace trim in two and machine stitching diagonally across the folded corner. Trim away the corner piece 0.5cm from stitching. Press seam edges open.

3 Pin two lace trims to the right side of the cross stitch panel forming a square frame. Overlap two corners and stitch together. Machine stitch trim to panel either side of the ribbon, pivoting at the corners.

PILLOWSLIP EDGING

Transform your bedlinen with this refreshing fuchsia and trellis design.

STITCHING INSTRUCTIONS

KEY PILLOWSLIP EDGING

DMC	Anchor	Madeira		Colour
3818	218	1405	● ●	DARK GREEN
471	265	1603	◖ ◖	PALE GREEN
718	88	0706	♥ ♥	DARK PINK
604	51	0614	· ·	PALE PINK
TRELLIS				
437	368	2011	● ●	BEIGE

STITCHING THE EDGING

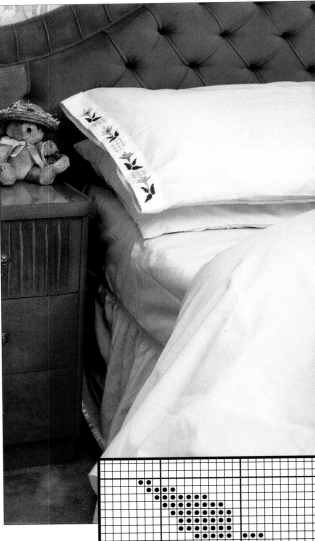

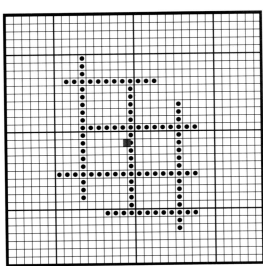

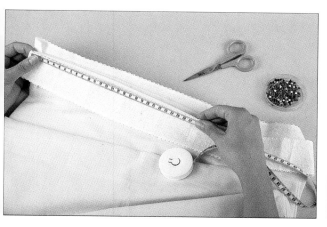

1 To complete the bedroom set of lampshade, cushion and picture frame, add co-ordinating bedlinen. Measure around the pillow slip opening, adding 4cm (1½in) seam allowance. Then, cut a piece of 5cm (2in) wide trimmed embroidery fabric to the correct length.

2 Divide the strip in half and starting from one end, cross stitch single fuchsias, alternating the colour of the flowers and using DMC cotton perle. Allow 28 holes, approximately 4cm (1½in) between each flower in which to add a trellis, again using DMC cotton perle.

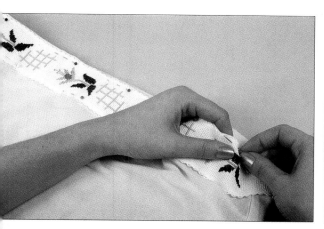

3 At the halfway point along the fabric, change direction and cross stitch the fuchsias facing the opposite way. Once completed, pin the trim to the pillowslip edge, turning the raw edges under 2cm at each end. Machine stitch in place along both sides. Add the same trim to the top sheet edge for a complete set.

4 For the top sheet, measure the width of the sheet, adding 4cm (1½in) for seam allowance. Then cut this length of embroidery trim and embroider the fuchsias and trellis alternating the shades of the flowers as you go. Machine stitch to the underside of the sheet so that when folded down, it will be on the top edge, so complementing the pillowcase design.

BUTTERFLY NAPKIN SET

A pastoral design to add a sophisticated touch to the dining table or a bit of style to a summer's picnic.

STITCHING INSTRUCTIONS

KEY NAPKINS

DMC	Anchor	Madeira		Colour
310	403	BLACK	■ ■	BLACK
554	108	802	O O	MAUVE
895	683	1314	◄ ◄	DARK GREEN
743	305	0109	J J	YELLOW
522	261	1513	▲ ▲	PALE GREEN
310	403	BLACK	☐	BLACK

STITCHING THE NAPKINS

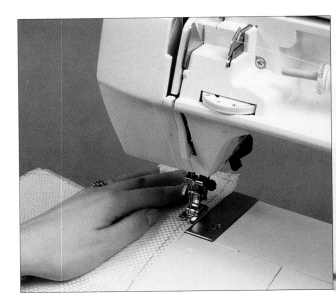

1 Cut a 30cm (11in) square at 11HPI Damask aida to match the table cloth. Tack around the square approximately 0.5cm from the edges using thread to match the fabric. Machine stitch along the tacking lines.

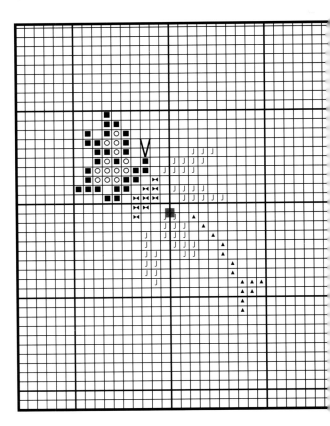

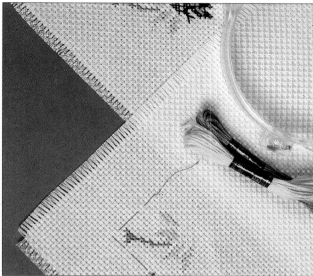

2 Gently pull the cloth threads from edges to create the fringe. Work each side separately, until the line of machine stitching is reached. Remove the tacking stitches before marking the corner to be embroidered, approximately 15 holes – 5cm (2in) – from one corner.

3 Following the chart, and using three strands of DMC stranded embroidery thread, start the stem at the corner. Complete with the butterfly, adding antennaes and French knots to finish (see the table cloth project overleaf, for French knot instructions).

MATCHING TABLE CLOTH

This matching cloth, together with the napkin set, makes a winning combination for creating a fresh table decoration.

STITCHING INSTRUCTIONS

KEY TABLE CLOTH

DMC	Anchor	Madeira		Colour
522	261	1513	J | J	PALE GREEN
895	683	1314	× | ×	DARK GREEN
310	403	BLACK	■ | ■	BLACK
554	108	0802	⊙ | ⊙	MAUVE
792	941	0914	► | ►	BLUE
743	305	0109	∩ | ∩	YELLOW
310	403	BLACK		BLACK

STITCHING THE TABLE CLOTH

1 To make a table cloth, use a wide fabric available by the metre, such as DMC's 11HPI Damask aida. For a rectangular or oval table, cut a piece approximately 65cm (26in) longer than the table. For a small circular table, cut a square of fabric. Prepare fabric edges for fringing by tacking and then machine stitching approximately 1cm from selvage.

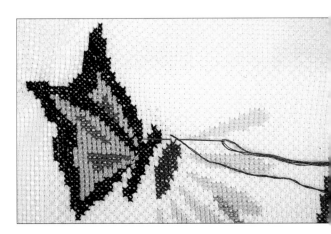

4 Continue the design, working each stitch individually. When changing colours, avoid trailing threads across the back of the work as they may snag or show through. Start again, weaving tail ends in as you go. Finish the butterfly with antennae made from two long stitches topped with French knots.

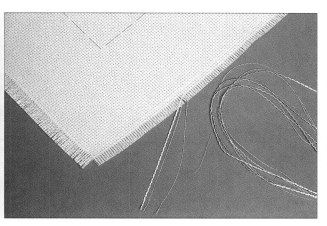

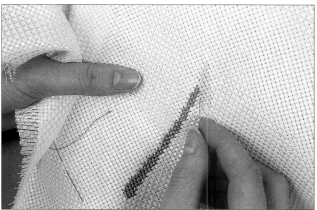

2 Fringe the edges by gently pulling threads away, until the line of machine stitching is reached. Work with two or three threads at a time and complete each side before starting the next. Tack marking lines approximately 12cm (4¾in) from each corner as guidelines for the cross stitch design.

3 Using three strands of embroidery thread, start the stem of the flower design at a point 11 holes – 4cm (1½in) – from the corner guidelines. Follow the chart for the flower and butterfly. To co-ordinate with your own dinner service, simply change the colours of the flower and butterfly to suit.

5 To make a French knot, start with the thread on the right side, hold thread firmly and wrap around the needle two or three times. Still holding the thread, insert needle close to the point it originally came from and pull through to the rear. The knot will stay in place.

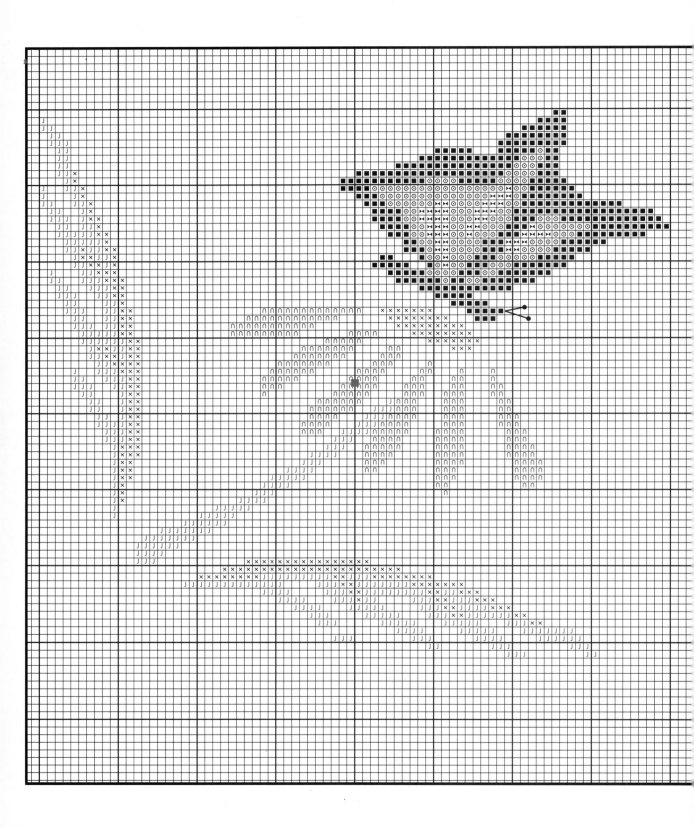

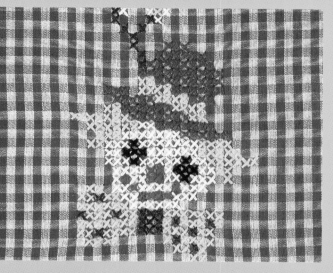

chapter 3
CHILDREN

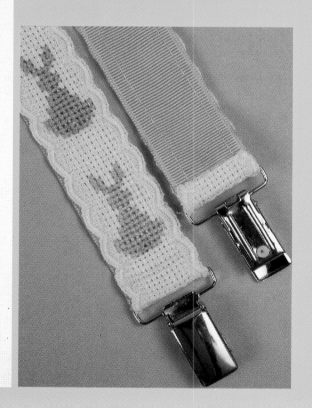

ADVENT CALENDAR

Count the days before Christmas in this great tradition - by stitching this festive wall-hanging, which will thrill children and adults alike!

STITCHING INSTRUCTIONS

KEY ADVENT CALENDAR

DMC	Anchor	Madeira		Colour
WHITE	1	WHITE	· ·	WHITE
310	BLACK	BLACK	■ ■	BLACK
971	316	0204	★ ★	ORANGE

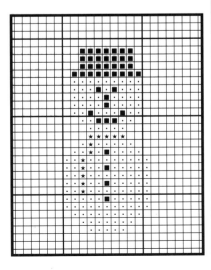

MAKING THE CALENDAR

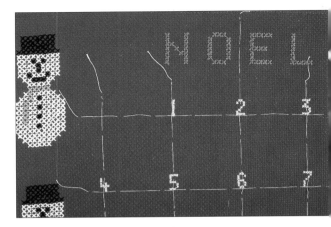

1 Cut a piece of bright red 14 HPI aida approximately 43cm wide x 54cm (17 x 21in) and machine stitch edges to prevent fraying. Using large running stitches, divide the fabric centre into 24 evenly spaced squares. With the 24th day at the foot, cross stitch each date on the relevant cross-piece of running stitches. Follow the chart to add four snowmen to either side, starting approximately 7cm (2¾in) from the top edge and 4cm (1½in) from the side.

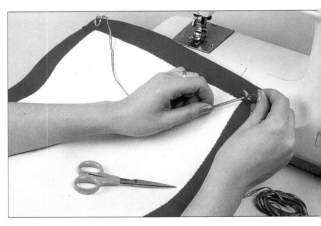

3 Machine stitch top approximately 2cm from edge to form a casing for a bamboo rod. Next add two curtain rings, one at either side, from which to hang the calendar. Alternatively, tie ribbon to the rings in order to form a pretty ribbon hanging.

2 Add the wording as desired, centred over the dates by counting the number of letters/stitches to be used, halve the total and count back from the centre to find start point. Once complete, cut a piece of heavyweight interfacing to approximately 35 x 48cm (13 x 19in) to form backing. Turn edges of aida over and slip stitch in place, adding weight to bottom corners if desired.

4 Using a further 24 curtain rings, add one to each of the cross stitched dates. Sew firmly in place just below the numbers, centrally when below double figures. Make up 24 little parcels, wrapping some in paper or netting to vary the choice.

5 Hang the little gifts, one to each ring, varying the selection and size for an even balance.

PINAFORE BIB

Create this novelty dress in a few simple steps.

STITCHING INSTRUCTIONS

KEY CLOWN FACE

DMC	Anchor	Madeira			Colour
11	WHITE	1	□	□	WHITE
742	303	0107	၆	၆	YELLOW
718	89	0707	●	●	PURPLE
797	123	0912	■	■	BLUE
666	9046	0510	#	#	RED
909	229	1303	○	○	GREEN

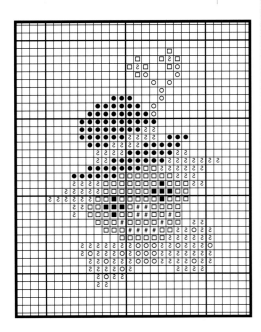

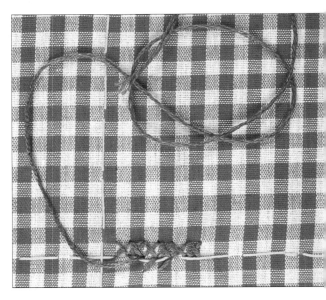

MAKING THE PINAFORE BIB

1 Cut a piece of gingham approximately 17 x 20cm (6¾ x 7¾in) which allows 3cm excess for easier handling. Mark the centre of the gingham, using long tacking stitches to define the design area. Using two strands of embroidery thread, begin the design.

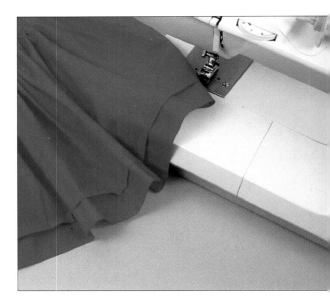

4 Make the trousers to complete the dungarees. Use a toddler's pattern and add elasticated cuffs. Alternatively, cuffs could be hemmed and turn up to show underside of denim. Make two buttonholes in ends of each strap.

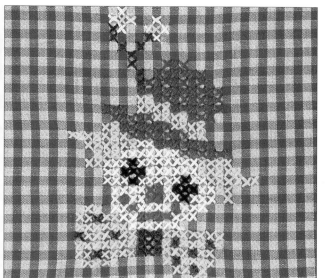

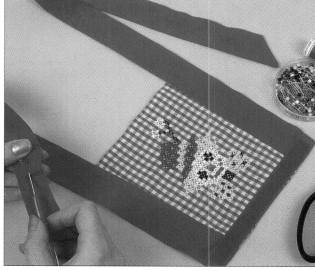

2 Following the chart, complete the motif, stitching four cross-stitches in each large gingham check. Once complete, trim the gingham to approximately 13 x 16cm (5 x 6⅜in). Add a denim backing, cut to the same size and machine stitch to gingham at top and bottom (right sides together). Turn and press.

3 Add the two straps, approximately 66cm (26in) long in matching denim. Fold in half and stitch one end and long edge, leaving last 16cm (6⅜in) open. Turn to right sides. Attach right side of unsewn strap end to right side of bib, stitch across end and side. Fold remaining strap edge back over to encase bib edge and slip stitch to finish.

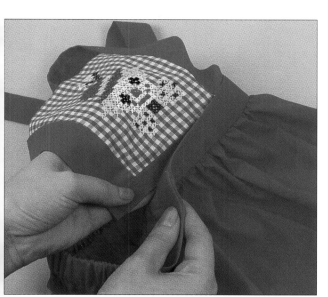

5 Add four poppas to inside waistband front and along bottom edge of bib, matching the positions. To join together, simply pop in place. Use the female sides of the poppa on trousers so that the stud will not press against body if bib is not worn. Finally, add buttons to back waistband.

DUNGAREE BIB

This bold bus design is a fun addition to any child's wardrobe.

STITCHING INSTRUCTIONS

KEY DUNGAREE BIB

DMC	Anchor	Madeira			Colour
666	9046	0510	#	#	RED
973	297	0105	·	·	YELLOW
WHITE	1	WHITE	☐	☐	WHITE
310	403	BLACK	■	■	BLACK

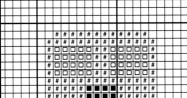

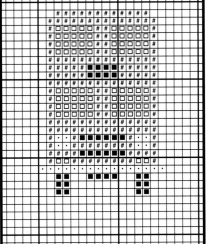

1 As with the little pinafore, cut a piece of gingham approximately 17 x 20cm (6¾ x 7¾in) which allows 3cm excess for handling. Mark the centre of the gingham, using long tacking stitches to define the design area. Using two strands of embroidery thread, begin the design.

4 Make the trousers to complete the dungarees. Use a toddler's pattern and add elasticated cuffs. Alternatively, cuffs could be hemmed and turn up to show underside of denim. Make two buttonholes in ends of each strap.

2 Following the chart, complete the motif, stitching four cross-stitches in each large gingham check. Once complete, trim the gingham to approximately 13 x 16cm (5 x 6⅜in). Add a denim backing, cut to the same size and machine stitch to gingham at top and bottom (right sides together). Turn and press.

3 Add the two straps, approximately 66cm (26in) long in matching denim. Fold in half and stitch one end and long edge, leaving last 16cm (6⅜in) open. Turn to right sides. Attach right side of unsewn strap end to right side of bib, stitch across end and side. Fold remaining strap edge back over to encase bib edge and slip stitch to finish.

5 Add four poppas to inside waistband front and along bottom edge of bib, matching the positions. To join together, simply pop in place. Use the female sides of the poppa on trousers so that the stud will not press against body if bib is not worn. Finally, add buttons to back waistband.

HAIRBAND AND BRACES

Matching accessories that add individual style to an outfit.

STITCHING INSTRUCTIONS

KEY HAIRBAND AND BRACES

DMC	Anchor	Madeira		Colour
954	241	1212	● ●	GREEN
927	399	1802	■ ■	GREY
605	25	0613	⊙ ⊙	PINK

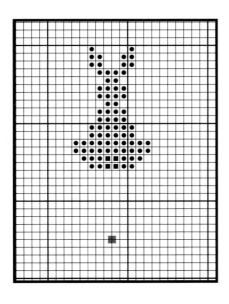

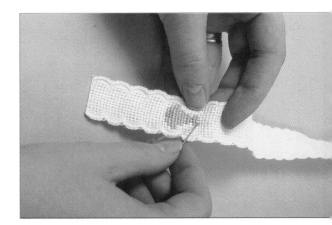

1 Using 0.25cm wide trim, cut a piece approximately 37.5cm (14¾in) in length for the headband. Start the cross stitch design following the chart, approximately 4.5cm (1¾in) from one raw edge. Begin with three strands of silver grey thread and cross stitch the bunny tail in the centre. Next, change to three strands of pink to complete the bunny design.

4 Feed the tube onto a child's hairband, working the design around to cover the full length. Work the braces in the same way, making each brace approximately 70cm (27½in) long. Finish both ends with brace clips.

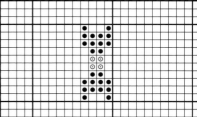

MAKING THE HAIRBAND AND BRACES

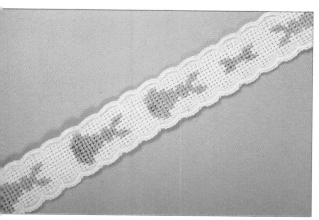

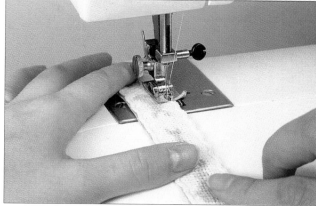

2 Start the next bunny, leaving 8 holes clear between each one, using pale green for the second body, changing back to pink for the third. Next, leave 5 holes before starting the centre bow design, using green for the bow and pink for the knot. Again leaving 5 holes clear, work three more bunnies with heads towards the centre and tails to the end, alternating pink and green for the bodies.

3 Cut a piece of 0.25cm wide grograin ribbon to the same length as the embroidered trim. Pin and then tack the two lengths, wrong sides together, turning in the short ends approximately 0.5cm to neaten. Machine stitch the two sides forming an open-ended tube.

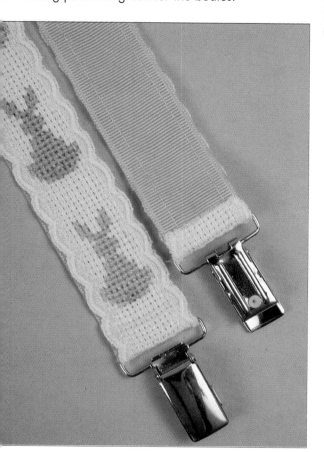

BIRTHDAY PICTURE

Choose a child's favourite character for the perfect birthday design.

STITCHING INSTRUCTIONS

KEY TRAIN

DMC	Anchor	Madeira			Colour
318	399	1802	◐	◐	GREY
413	236	1713	◖	◖	DARK GREY
666	9046	0510	#	#	RED
972	303	0107	·	·	YELLOW
820	134	0913	●	●	ROYAL BLUE
WHIITE	1	WHITE	☐	☐	WHITE
762	234	1803	☉	☉	PALE GREY
310	403	BLACK	■	■	BLACK

MAKING THE BIRTHDAY PICTURE

TIP
Use alphabet and numerical charts for name and dates, page 11.

3 Once the design is complete, stitch the train's face using just one strand of thread and backstitch for the eyes, nose and mouth. If a different design is preferred for a girl, substitute the house chart (page 78) or clown face (page 40). Start the design roughly in the middle, at the centre of the running stitches.

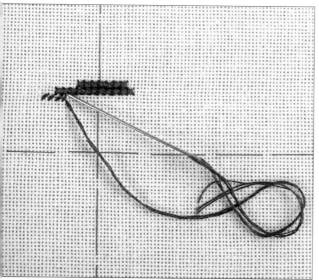

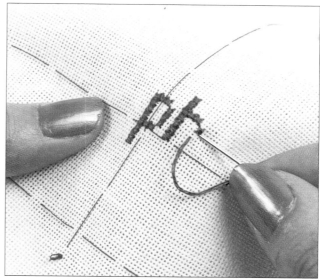

1 Using very fine evenweave embroidery linen, cut a piece 26 x 34cm (10 x 13in). Tack the edge and mark the centre with large running stitches. Follow the chart, and using three strands of DMC embroidery thread, begin the design working in short rows. Again with running stitches, mark the position of the two lines of wording (approximately 3cm/1¼in apart).

2 To centre the wording within the picture, work out how many stitches (and spaces) are required for the name and date, halve the total and then start the cross stitch at this halfway point, at the centre of the running stitch made earlier. Using three strands of thread, work each letter individually to avoid threads carried from one letter to another showing through.

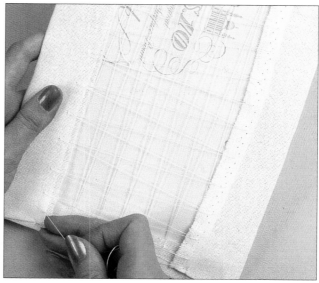

4 To mount the finished work, cut a piece of wadding to 22 x 27cm (8 x 10in) and glue it to a piece of mounting card (available from art shops) cut to the same size. Fold the edges of the fabric over the card, ensuring the design is in the centre.

5 To secure in place, lace the fabric with strong thread, from top to bottom and side to side. Place in a picture frame (with or without glass) and add the back and strut. For this design we've used a 10in x 8in picture frame.

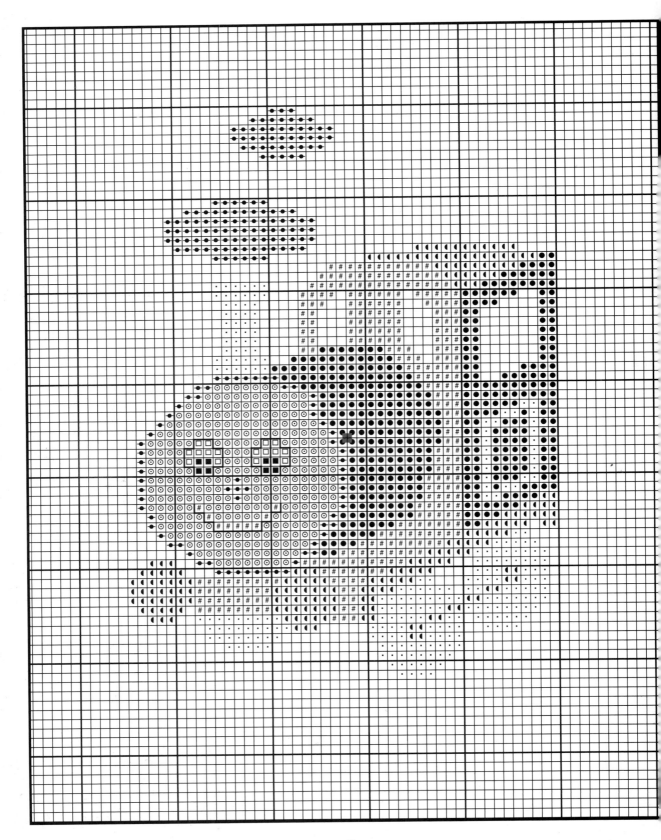

chapter 4
KITCHEN

JAR LACIES

Add a finishing touch to home-made preserves for the ideal gift.

STITCHING INSTRUCTIONS

KEY JAR LACIES

DMC	Anchor	Madeira		Colour
817	19	0211	■ ■	RED
9486	245	1404	× ×	GREEN
WHITE	1	WHITE	· ·	WHITE
444	290	0105	★ ★	YELLOW

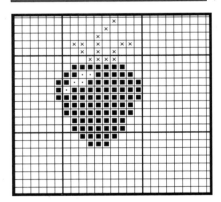

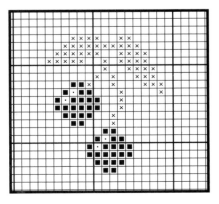

STITCHING THE JAR LACIES

1 Jar lacies add an attractive top to home made preserves as well as neatly identifying the flavouring. A printed check on plain weave cotton is ideal for cross stitching and practical for this project. Lace edging and 1cm wide ribbon adds a pretty finish. Using a 25cm (9in) square of fabric, mark a circle (using a plate or saucer) approximately 16cm (6⅜in) in diameter. Next divide the circle into equal quarters with contrasting tacking thread.

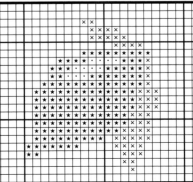

4 Trim the edge under approximately 0.4-0.5cm and pin the pre-gathered lace trim to the underside, over the turned edge. Work around the pot cover, until the lace ends meet. Overlap the lace edging approximately 1cm, turning the upper edge over so that the right side remains neat. Tack and then machine stitch the lace to the fabric all around the circumference.

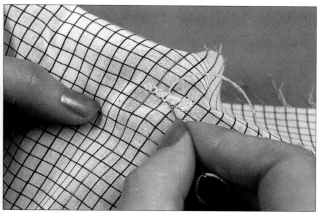

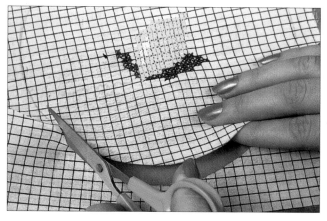

2 Using three strands of DMC stranded cotton, start each design – choose from lemon, strawberry or cherries. Stitch four cross stitches in each printed square and work in short rows to complete each design. When changing colours, fasten off and start again, rather than carry thread across the back of different coloured stitches, as this may show through and thus spoil the design.

3 Once the whole design is completed, trim around the edge of the circle along the outline previously drawn. It is advisable to use small, sharp embroidery scissors which will give greater control on small items and thus help achieve a neat circular edge.

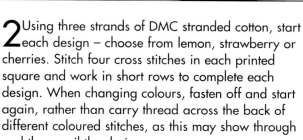

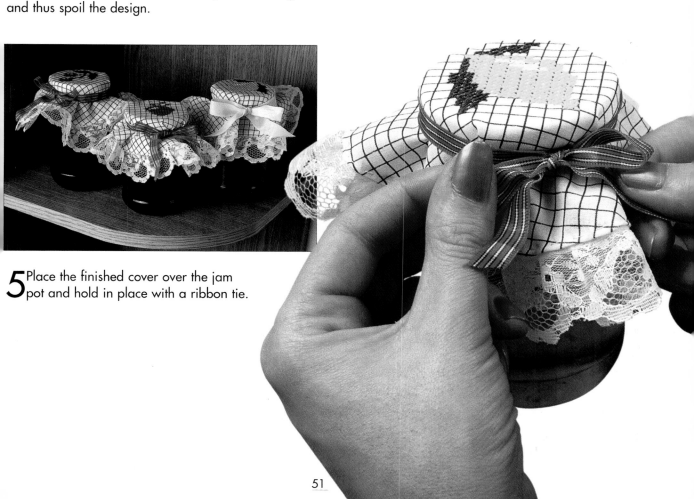

5 Place the finished cover over the jam pot and hold in place with a ribbon tie.

CAFE STYLE CURTAINS

How to add a continental feel to your kitchen.

STITCHING INSTRUCTIONS

KEY CAFE CURTAINS

DMC	Anchor	Madeira		Colour
700	228	1305	◆ ◆	GREEN

STITCHING THE CURTAINS

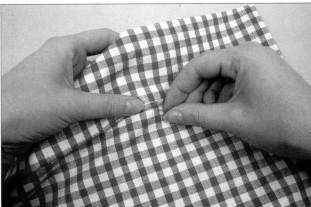

3 To finish the curtain, turn in side seams 1cm and again 1.5cm encasing raw edges. The cross stitch border should now be on the edge. Machine side seams. Press to form crisp edge. Turn up hem, leaving 2.5cm/1in (5 checks) between border and hemline. Turn raw edge under again and hem in place, using either hemming stitch or iron-on wondaweb.

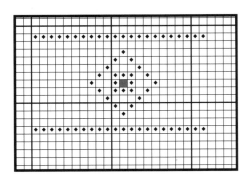

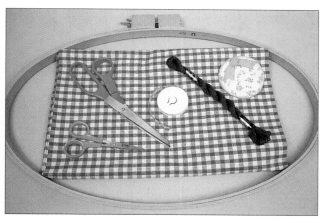

1 A cafe style curtain is particularly suited to gingham, an evenweave check fabric. Measure your window, adding 5cm (2in) to the width measure for side and seams, and select the depth required, again add an extra 6cm (2⅜in)for top seam and 10cm (4in) for deep hem. (Cafe curtains are usually hung halfway down the window.)

2 Using the embroidery hoop to hold the fabric taut whilst stitching, begin the design approximately 12.5cm (5in) from lower edge (19 checks) and 2.5cm (1in) from side (5 checks). Following the relevant charts from the chart section and using DMC cotton perle, work the borders in rows of cross stitch. Then stitch the motifs, working each stitch individually.

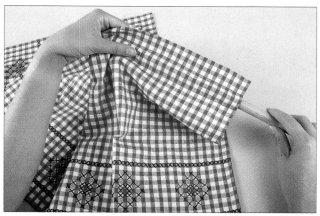

4 Finish the top of the curtain by turning in the upper edge approximately 7cm (2¾in) along the edge of the checked pattern. Turn the raw edge under again and machine stitch in place, following edge of checks on right side for invisible stitching. To create the casing for wooden pole, machine stitch invisible stitching. To create the casing for wooden pole, machine stitch another row, from side to side, 2.5cm/1in (5 checks) from top edge.

5 Cut a 1cm diameter wooden pole to the width of the window recess. Try it for size before inserting it between the top two rows of machine stitching. Adjust the curtain along the pole so that any gathers are even.

NAPKIN RINGS

This geometric design can be used to enhance a variety of tablewear - adding an individual touch to every meal.

STITCHING INSTRUCTIONS

KEY NAPKIN RINGS

DMC	Anchor	Madeira		Colour
700	228	1305	◆ ◆	GREEN

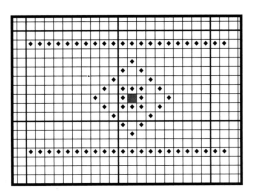

MAKING THE NAPKIN RINGS

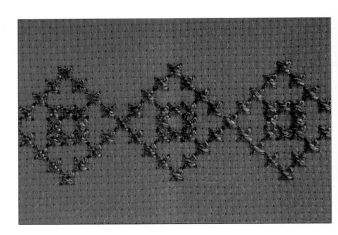

1 Cut a strip of 14 HPI aida approximately 6cm wide x 17cm (2½ x 6¾in) long. Starting 1cm from one of the short edges, start the design (following the chart) and using DMC cotton perle. Work each cross of the stitch over 2 holes of the aida and stitch each cross stitch individually.

4 With right sides facing, pin short ends of aida and gingham together to form a ring, matching motifs. Machine stitch and then press the seam edges open.

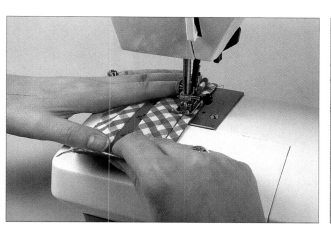

2 Repeat the motif along the strip of aida, using one point stitch as a common stitch for two motifs. Cut two strips of gingham on the bias, approximately 3cm (1½in) wide and 17cm (6¾in) long. With right sides together, machine stitch one piece to the aida along the top approximately 1cm from edge. Repeat for lower edge.

3 Fold the gingham back along the stitching so right sides show, press for crisp firm edge. Repeat on lower edge. Turn in again, encasing raw edges and press, do not sew. Open out gingham.

5 Finally, working from the wrong side, fold the gingham bias strips over the raw edges of top and bottom of the napkin ring and slip stitch to the aida.

MATCHING NAPKIN

An inexpensive way to co-ordinate stitching designs for your tablewear.

STITCHING INSTRUCTIONS

KEY MATCHING NAPKIN

DMC	Anchor	Madeira		Colour
700	228	1305	◆ ◆	GREEN

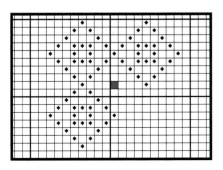

MAKING THE NAPKIN

1 Cut two triangular pieces of red aida, each approximately 11 x 11 x 15.5cm (4 x 4 x 6in) with which to make the corner decorative pieces for the napkins. Starting at the short point, approximately 2cm from edge, begin the diamond cross stitch design.

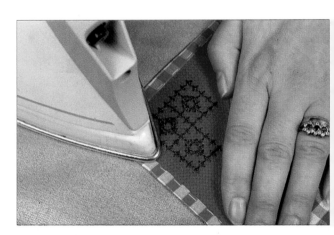

4 Fold in the gingham edge approximately 0.5cm around the whole napkin and then again to encase the raw edge and edge of decorative corner pieces. Tack in place and gently press to hold edges before stitching.

2 Continue cross stitching the motif, so that the left and right edges of the first diamond form part of the next two diamonds. Cut the napkins from gingham, approximately 34cm (13½in) square.

3 Turn in 0.5cm of the lower (longest) edge of the cross stitched aid triangles, tack in place and press firmly with a warm iron. Pin and tack the triangles to two opposite corners of napkin, leaving approximately 1cm of gingham edge to fold back over as edging.

5 Carefully machine stitch the turned in edge all around the napkin to neaten edges. Also stitch across the outer edge of the aida triangle to the napkin. Remove tacking stitches. Press firmly with a damp press cloth and hot iron. The napkin is now ready to slip into the napkin ring.

POT HOLDER

Protect your hands with this practical cloth - which will also look cheery when hung up beside the oven.

STITCHING INSTRUCTIONS

KEY POT HOLDER

DMC	Anchor	Madeira		Colour
700	228	1305	♦ ♦	GREEN

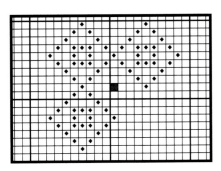

MAKING THE POT HOLDER

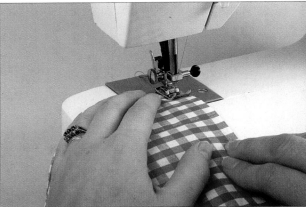

3 Pin the padded backing to the aida, wrong sides together. Tack and stitch in place. Cut strips of gingham on the bias, approximately 2.5cm (1in) wide. Join together to form one strip 68cm (26½in) long. Starting at one corner, pin one edge of the strip to the aida side of the pot holder. Tack in place, turning at the corners.

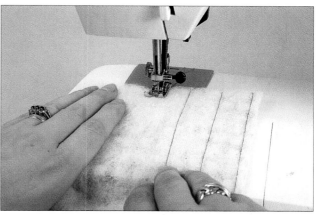

1 Cut a piece of aida approximately 17cm (6¾in) square to make the pot holder. Starting in the centre of the piece, cross stitch the design, repeating the diamond pattern four times (see the chart on page 54). Add a single cross stitch in the centre to complete the pattern.

2 Cut a piece of gingham and a piece of 0.5cm thick wadding the same size as the aida, approximately 17cm (6¾in) square. Attach the wadding and gingham to form the heat resistant backing, by machine stitching the two fabrics together at approximately 2.5cm (1in) intervals.

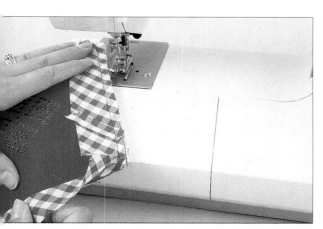

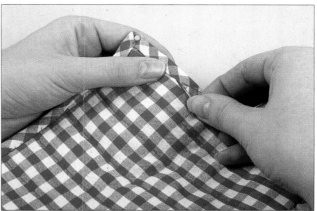

4 Make a loop from gingham approximately 9 x 2.5cm (3½ x 1in). Stitch the long edge, turn through and press. Attach the loop to one corner of the pad, slipping ends under the gingham trim. Machine stitch the trim to the pad, including loop ends.

5 Once all sides have been machine stitched, press using a dry press cloth. Fold the trim over along the stitching. Fold over again to encase raw edges and then turn under the trim edge and slip stitch to the back of the pad.

KITCHEN ROLLER BLIND

A fresh decorative finish for an everyday blind.

STITCHING INSTRUCTIONS

KEY KITCHEN BLIND

DMC	Anchor	Madeira		Colour
700	228	1305	◆ ◆	GREEN

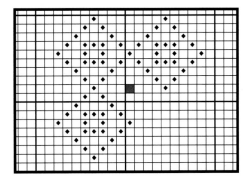

STITCHING THE ROLLER BLIND

1 Measure the window recess accurately in order to determine width and length of the blind. Ensure the fabric chosen is at least 5cm (2in) wider and 20cm (7in) longer than the recess to allow for hems. Cut a length of gingham for the trim approximately 20cm (7in) wide.

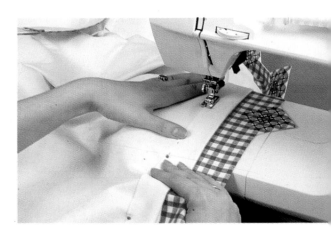

4 Turn work to the right sides, press firmly for crisp edge. Next, pin, tack and stitch the main fabric for the blind to the top of the edge of the trim, right sides together. Open out and press to form a crisp edge. Working on the right side, again machine stitch through all thicknesses approximately 3cm (1¼in) from edge to form the pocket for the blind lath.

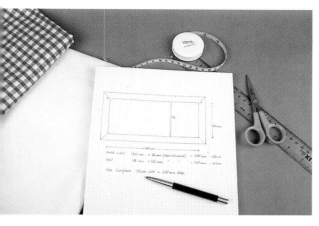

2 Starting at the centre of the gingham, cross stitch the diamond design. Repeat the design either side of the centre diamond, leaving 7 gingham checks between each design.

3 Stiffen the gingham trim by ironing fusible interfacing on the wrong side. Leave to cool. Pin and tack a piece of the main fabric, approximately 14cm (5½in) wide, to the trim, with right sides together. Machine stitch, starting at one edge level with the centre of the cross stitch diamonds. Stitch around each design, pivoting at the bottom. Trim seam allowance and clip corners.

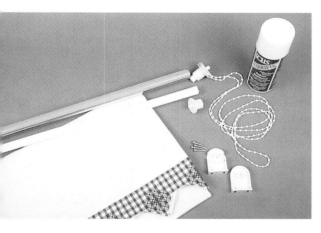

5 Hem each side of the blind by turning in approximately 2.5cm (1in) either side and machine stitching. (The fabric width should be 1.2cm less than the blind roller width.) Neaten raw edges of the top by overstitching or turning under the hemming. Spray with fabric stiffener and attach to a purchased blind kit following manufacturer's instructions.

TEATIME TRAY CLOTH

Complement this tea tray cloth with this versatile design.

STITCHING INSTRUCTIONS

KEY TRAY CLOTH

DMC	Anchor	Madeira		Colour
700	228	1305	◆ ◆	GREEN

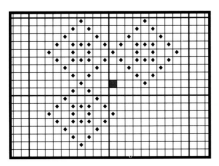

STITCHING THE TRAY CLOTH

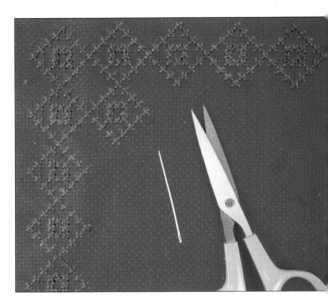

1 Cut pieces of 14HPI aida and gingham to fit the tea tray. Work the design in one corner of the aida, approximately 3.5cm (1⅜in) from the edge. Cross stitch 5 diamonds along one edge. At right angles to the first row, work another 4 diamonds and to finish, add another diamond at the corner.

4 Fold the binding again to encase the raw edges of the tray cloth. Turn under the remaining raw edge of the binding strip and then slip stitch to the underside of the tray cloth. Press again, using a damp press cloth and hot iron.

 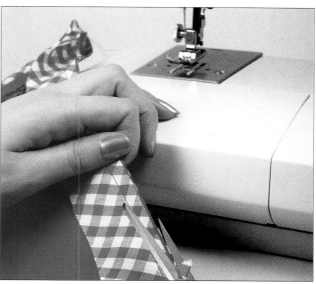

2 Working with the wrong sides together, pin the aida to the gingham so that all sides match. Machine stitch to hold in place. Prepare the gingham trim by cutting strips of gingham on the bias approximately 4cm wide. Join end to end until the strip is long enough to encase the tray cloth edges.

3 Start at one corner and working with right sides together, pin, tack and then machine stitch the gingham binding to the tray cloth, turning at corners. Trim seam allowances to a scant 0.5cm all around. Fold binding back along stitching line. Press.

TIMELY TEA COSY

Complete the linen set by stitching this stylish teapot cosy.

STITCHING INSTRUCTIONS

KEY TEA COSY

DMC	Anchor	Madeira		Colour
700	228	1305	◆ ◆	GREEN

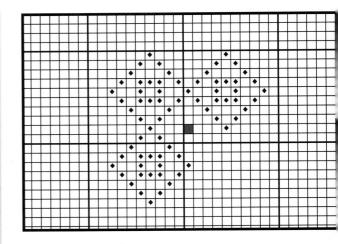

MAKING THE TEA COSY

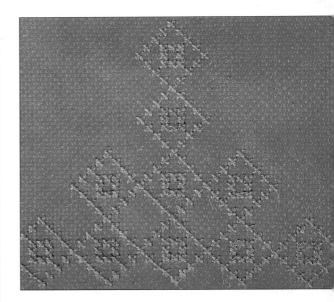

1 Cut a piece of aida approximately 28 x 34cm (11 x 13in). Starting at the centre, approximately 3cm (1¼in) from the lower edge, cross stitch the first diamond, using DMC cotton perle. Repeat the design, working four diamonds each side of the centre, joining the diamonds using one side stitch as a common stitch between diamonds.

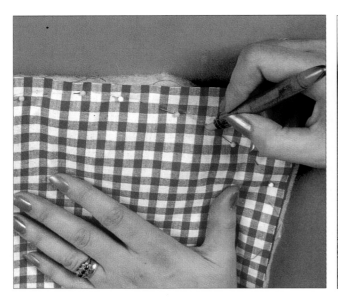

2 Once the design is complete, sandwich the aida between wadding and gingham, with right side facing the gingham. Mark the tea cosy shape onto the gingham, starting at the centre. Machine stitch the bottom edge only. Make the back of the tea cosy in the same way. Trim stitched edges to within 0.5cm of stitching, turn to encase wadding.

3 Next, pin the three layers together and machine stitch around remaining edges. Pin both front and back together, matching stitching lines, and with right sides showing. Tack in place. Add the gingham binding by cutting strips of gingham on the bias approximately 3.5cm (1 3/8in) wide. Join together to create a length that will encase cosy edges. Tack one edge to the right side of the cosy, over the stitching lines.

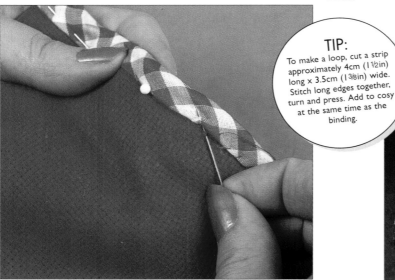

TIP:
To make a loop, cut a strip approximately 4cm (1 1/2in) long x 3.5cm (1 3/8in) wide. Stitch long edges together, turn and press. Add to cosy at the same time as the binding.

5 Fold the binding over to the back, encasing the edges. Turn remaining raw edge under again and pin to back of cosy. Slip stitch in place to finish, also encasing the other loop end at the top of the cosy.

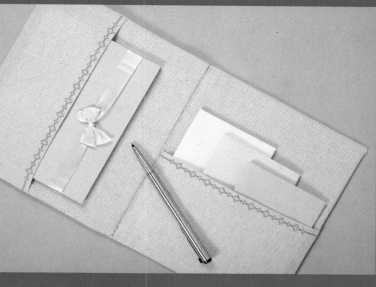

chapter 5
GIFTS

GIFT TAGS

STITCHING INSTRUCTIONS

KEY GIFT TAGS

DMC	Anchor	Madeira			Colour
797	123	0912	×	×	BLUE
352	9	0303	○	○	PEACH
905	258	1413	ﻌ	ﻌ	GREEN
760	895	0813	●	●	PINK
562	205	1213	#	#	GREEN

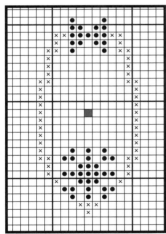

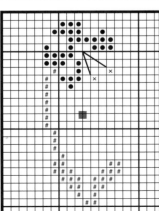

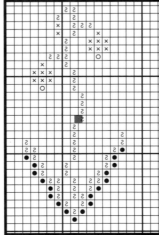

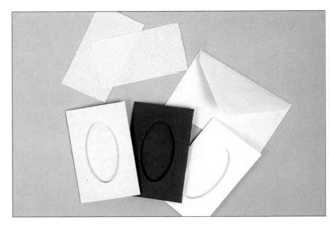

1 Personalised gift tags add a very individual touch to any present, either as a finishing touch to a handcrafted gift or a more personal feel on a purchased one. Select suitable gift cards with cut outs, readily available from art/craft shops. Cut 11HPI pearl aida approximately 3cm (1 ¼ in) larger than card size to allow for handling.

4 Centre the design, right side down, over the hole, using the left flap as backing. Trim away any excess aida that overlaps the card edge. Carefully open card, holding design in place on left flap now right side up. Gently lift edges and glue or tape in place to hold securely.

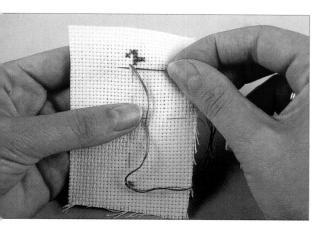

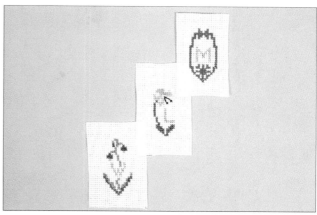

2 Tack around the design area and then choose the design and initial (chosen from the alphabet chart on page 10) suitable for the occasion. Mark the centre of the design area with tacking thread. Using three strands of stranded cotton, either start at the top or at the centre, working each stitch separately.

3 Continue working the design, following the chart and counting holes and stitches to ensure the spacing is accurate. Once the motif and initial has been completed, gently press the pieces, using a soft towel surface and dry press cloth. Once cool, trim to approximately 0.5cm smaller than the card size.

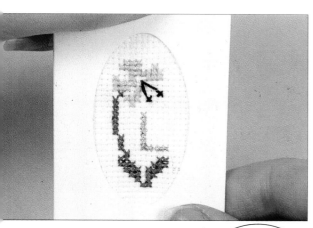

5 If using glue, wait until it has dried before the next application. Alternatively, use double-sided tape around the edges of the card and cut out. Fold the left flap over the window and press firmly around the edges to secure.

TIP
Extra pressing between books can help to secure the card and design in place if glue is reluctant to hold.

WRITING CASE AND SPECTACLES CASE

MAKING THE WRITING CASE

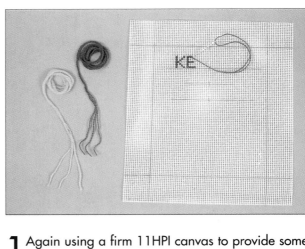

STITCHING INSTRUCTIONS

KEY BOTH CASES

DMC	Anchor	Madeira		Colour
3689	74	0607	■ ■	PINK
3803	65	0602	★ ★	BIRGUNDY

1 Again using a firm 11HPI canvas to provide some support, cut the canvas to the desired size, approximately 25cm wide x 30cm (9 x 11in). Using a pencil, mark the outer edge of the front panel, approximately 20 x 23cm (7 x 9in). Mark a central line from top to bottom and then mark the placement lines for the wording. Three lines have been used in this project, each separated by two squares with each letter standing 7 squares high. (Use the alphabet chart on page 11 to select wording.)

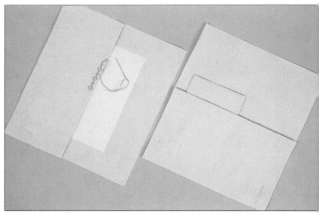

4 Cut the lining pieces from 14 HPI grey fabric, adding two half size pieces for stationery pockets. Turn in 1cm on inner edge of pockets and press firmly with steam iron. Cross stitch the inner border pattern from the cover, holding the turned edge in place. Machine stitch the pockets in place, leaving the decorative edge free.

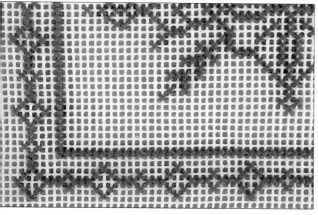

2 Calculate the word spacing by counting number of stitches and spaces in each letter/word. Halve the total in each line and count back from the centre to find starting point. Then using one strand of 3-ply yarn, cross stitch the chosen wording. Next, stitch around the marked border, using the dark rose yarn to match the lettering and following the chart.

TIP
If desired, repeat the front design, without wording, for the back cover of the case.

3 Work the motif in the centre, five rows from the border. Then fill in the centre panel with one strand of pink 3 ply yarn. Stitch the letters and outer edge of main motif and in the centre of the border motif. Finish the design with contrasting soft grey to completely fill the motif and outer edge of the case.

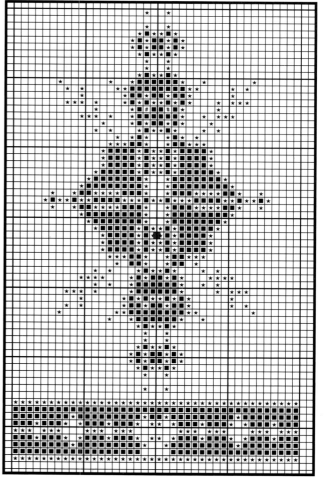

5 Machine stitch the outer front piece to the inside front and outer back to inside back, working with right sides together. Leave open at spine. Turn to right sides and press gently. Insert card, cut to size, between the two layers of front and back. Turn in the spine edges to neaten and slip stitch the back to front to form the case.

WRITING CASE AND SPECTACLES CASE CONTINUED.

Using the same chart and key as the writing case (on the previous page no. 71).

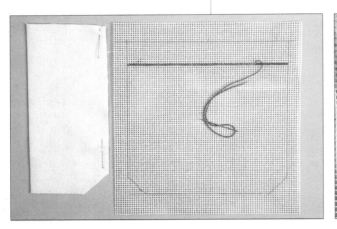

1 To provide reasonable protection, we have used a firm 11HPI canvas for the spectacles case. Cut the canvas to approximately 21cm wide x 22cm (8¼ x 8¾ in) and then mark the outline of the case with a pencil. Begin the first row of the cross stitch design, using one strand of 3-ply wool and following the chart.

2 Continue to fill in the design on both sides of the case, completing the motif outline in the darker thread, before adding the pale pink and soft grey stitches. Once complete, prepare the case lining, cut from cotton poplin. Cut the lining to the same size as the canvas outline.

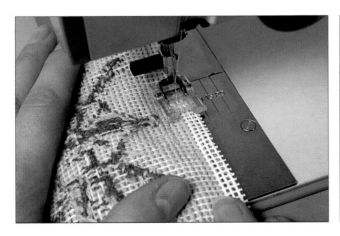

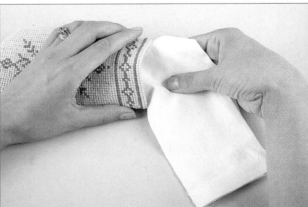

3 Fold the lining in half and machine stitch around the shaped ends and side seam. Press well. Working with right sides together, fold the completed canvas in half and machine stitch the shaped end and side. Turn to right sides and press gently, using a dry press cloth and warm iron.

4 Fit the lining into the case so that seams match and the wrong sides of lining and case are together. Turn in the top opening of both case and lining by approximately 1cm.

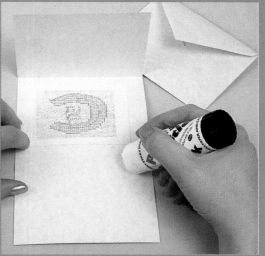

chapter 6
CARDS

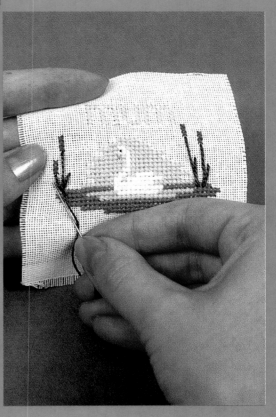

HAPPY BIRTHDAY CARDS

Personalised cards that will make lasting impressions.

STITCHING INSTRUCTIONS

KEY BIRTHDAY CARDS

DMC	Anchor	Madeira			Colour
CAR					
666	9046	0510	#	#	RED
928	1708	3948	♥	♥	PALE GREY
310	403	BLACK	■	■	BLACK
444	291	0105	○	○	YELLOW
SWAN					
3826	349	2009	○	○	BROWN
966	203	1209	J	J	GREEN
825	147	0912	#	#	BRIGHT BLUE
3761	160	0908	○	○	PALE BLUE
977	304	0203	◆	◆	ORANGE
310	403	BLACK	●	●	BLACK
WHITE	1	WHITE			WHITE

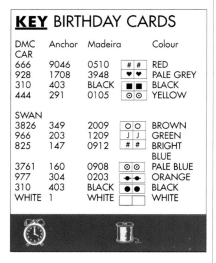

STITCHING THE CARDS

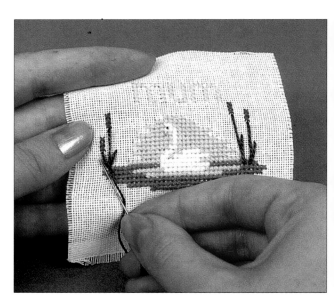

1 Choose a suitable design for the person; these projects show a swan among bullrushes for Mum and a colourful car for Dad. Cross stitch the design (following the relevant charts), onto a piece of 11HPI aida approximately 2cm larger than the card window.

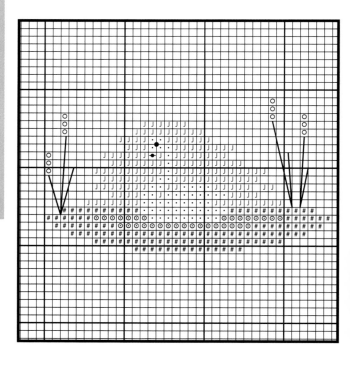

2 Position the completed design over the cut-out hole of the card and gently mark the corners on the wrong side. Trim away any excess fabric, leaving approximately 1cm all around to attach to the card.

3 Again, position the design over the hole, making sure it is central and square within the window. Dab a little glue to each corner to hold in place before adding strips of glue to the left hand flap and along the design edges. Close the flap over the design and press firmly together.

CHRISTMAS CARDS AND TAGS

Stitch a festive card and gift tag to add that finishing touch to your presents.

STITCHING INSTRUCTIONS

KEY CHRISTMAS CARDS

DMC	Anchor	Madeira		Colour
666	9046	0510	# #	RED
986	246	1314	♥ ♥	DARK GREEN
444	290	0105	● ●	YELLOW
648	398	1902	○ ○	GREY

MAKING THE CARDS

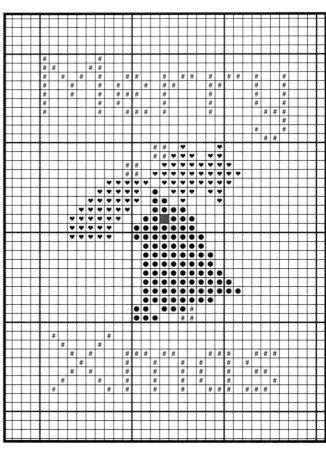

1 Cut a piece of 11HPI aida approximately the same size as the folded card. Mark the centre of the fabric with running stitches in order to position the design. Stitch the chosen festive message by following the charts, using three strands of embroidery thread.

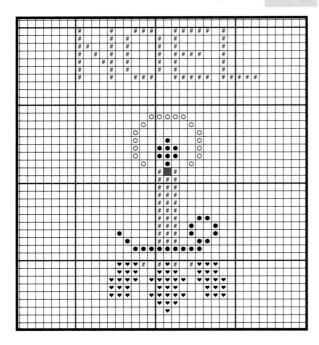

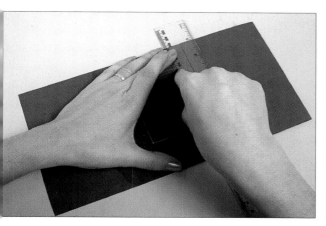

2 To make your own cards, cut a piece of card (available from art shops) 30 x 15cm (11 x 6in). Gently score two fold lines 10cm apart and fold both in to the centre. On the centre panel, mark the window area approximately 6 x 8cm (2 x 3in) starting 3cm (1¼in) from the top edge and 4cm from the bottom edge. Carefully draw a border approximately 0.3cm from the pencilled edge, using a contrasting colour, before cutting out the window.

3 Place the completed design over the cut-out, leaving a selvage for gluing, trim away any excess fabric. Dab glue on to each corner and press firmly to hold in place. Add strips of glue around the sides of the left flap of the card, plus strips along the outer edge of the aida. Close the flap over the design and press together, leaving under a weight to dry.

SPECIAL OCCASION CARDS

Make a unique card to commemorate a special occasion.

STITCHING INSTRUCTIONS

KEY COTTAGE CARD

DMC	Anchor	Madeira			Colour
995	410	1102	◖	◖	ELECTRIC BLUE
3827	363	2209	⋈	⋈	LIGHT TAN
775	976	1001	●	●	DARK BLUE
349	13	0212	·	·	RED
701	227	1305	★	★	FERN GREEN
420	370	2214	⊙	⊙	BROWN
310	403	BLACK	Ǝ	Ǝ	BLACK

KEY SNOWFLAKE CARD

DMC	Anchor	Madeira			Colour
791	149	0914	●	●	DARK BLUE
747	928	1104	×	×	LIGHT BLUE

MAKING THE CARDS

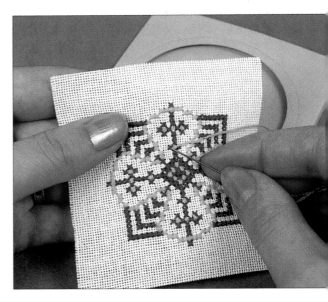

1 Whether for moving to a new home or as a simple thank you, an individually stitched card can become a treasured memento. Cut a small piece of 11HPI aida approximately 2cm larger than the folded card size. Following the charts and using three strands of embroidery thread, complete each design in the centre of the aida.

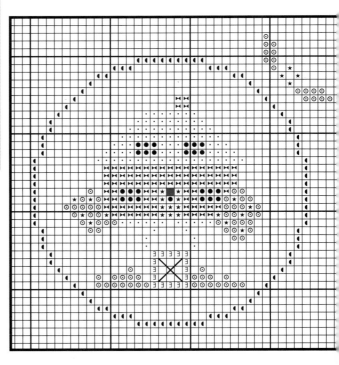

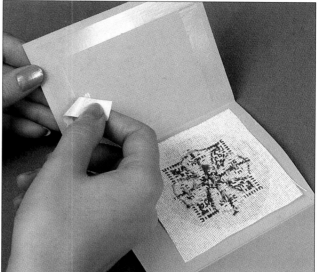

2 To emphasise particular areas, such as the chimney or window frames of the house, use a single strand of embroidery thread and simple back stitch to outline the feature desired. Then place the finished piece over the cut out hole, pencil mark four points around the edge and trim away excess aida, leaving a border approximately 1cm all around.

3 Place trimmed piece over the window, face down and whilst holding in place, lift each of the corners and add a dab of glue to hold securely. Using double sided tape (or glue), tape around all edges of the left flap of card as well as along the edges of the aida. Close the flap over the design and press firmly in place.

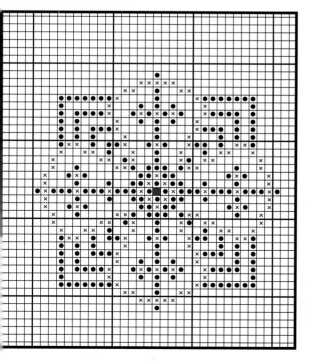

ACKNOWLEDGEMENTS

Stranded Cotton
Aida and Damask Linen - DMC Creative World Ltd
Anchor Embroidery thread - Coats Leisure Crafts Group

BIBLIOGRAPHY

Cross Stitch Designs – Kate Greenaway (David & Charles)
Cross Stitch Design Manual – Fran Rose (David & Charles)
The Cross Stitch and Sampler Book – Liz Mundle and John Eaton
(Apple Press)

THIS BOOK
BELONGS T

C000018916

Name: Age:

Favourite player:

2017-2018
My Predictions...   Actual...

Canaries' final position:

Canaries' top scorer:

Championship winners:

Championship top scorer:

FA Cup winners:

Carabao Cup winners:

Contributors: Rob Mason & Peter Rogers.

A TWOCAN PUBLICATION

©2017. Published by twocan under licence from Norwich City FC.

ISBN: 978-1-911502-26-5

£10

3

CONTENTS

The Squad 2017-18	**6**
Double Acts: Bruce & Watson	16
Nélson Oliveira Poster	**18**
Six Steps: Darren Huckerby	19
Championship Key Players	**20**
What Ball?	24
Marley Watkins Poster	**25**
Who are Ya?	26
Training to Win	**28**
Ivo Pinto Poster	30
Football 50 Wordsearch	**31**
Squad Photograph	32
Player of the Year	**34**
Former Players of the Year	35
Six Steps: Wes Hoolahan	**36**
Wes Hoolahan Poster	37
Championship Challenge	**38**
James Maddison Poster	42
Six Steps: Grant Holt	**43**
World Cup Quiz	44
Double Acts: Crook & Goss	**46**
Make Your Own Foosball Team	48
Angus Gunn Poster	**49**
Christmas Crackers	50
Fan'tastic	**52**
Yanic Wildschut Poster	54
Made in Norwich: Danny Mills	**55**
Home Turf	56
2017-18 Predictions	**58**
Made in Norwich: Todd Cantwell	60
Josh Murphy Poster	**61**
Answers	62

ANGUS GUNN

1
GOALKEEPER

NATIONALITY: English **DOB:** 22/01/1996

DID YOU KNOW: Angus, the son of iconic City stopper Bryan, started his career in Norwich's Academy before joining Manchester City. He is now on a season-long loan from the Citizens.

IVO PINTO

2
DEFENDER

NATIONALITY: Portuguese **DOB:** 07/01/1990

DID YOU KNOW: Before joining the Canaries, the marauding full-back made over 100 appearances for Dinamo Zagreb, helping them win consecutive Croatian titles, as well as Croatian Cup and Super Cup successes.

JAMES HUSBAND

3
DEFENDER

NATIONALITY: English **DOB:** 03/01/1994

DID YOU KNOW: James arrived at Carrow Road in the summer of 2017, having spent three years in the North East at Boro's Riverside Stadium.

RUSSELL MARTIN **5**
DEFENDER

NATIONALITY: Scottish   **DOB:** 04/01/1986

DID YOU KNOW: Skipper Russell Martin has been a Canary since January 2010 after making his loan move from Peterborough United a permanent one and has now played over 300 games for Norwich City.

HARRISON **REED** **4**
MIDFIELDER

NATIONALITY: English   **DOB:** 27/01/1995

DID YOU KNOW: Harrison, a product of the Saints' Academy, joined City on a season-long loan deal from Southampton before the start of 2017-18 campaign.

STEVEN NAISMITH **7** MIDFIELDER

NATIONALITY: Scottish   **DOB:** 14/09/1986

DID YOU KNOW: Scotland international Steven started his career with over a hundred appearances for Kilmarnock, before joining Scottish giants Rangers, where he won three Premiership titles, two Scottish Cups and three Scottish League Cups.

CHRISTOPH ZIMMERMANN **6** DEFENDER

NATIONALITY: German   **DOB:** 12/01/1993

DID YOU KNOW: Christoph followed Head Coach Daniel Farke from Borussia Dortmund II in July 2017, joining the Canaries on a free transfer.

MARIO VRANČIĆ **8** MIDFIELDER

NATIONALITY: Bosnian   **DOB:** 23/05/1989

DID YOU KNOW: Mario was born in the city of Slavonski Brod in what was formerly known as Yugoslavia, before moving to Germany with his family at the age of five. He has played for his adopted nation at youth levels, but now represents his homeland's senior side.

NÉLSON OLIVEIRA   **9** FORWARD

NATIONALITY: Portuguese   **DOB:** 08/08/1991

DID YOU KNOW: Nélson scored on his Champions League debut for Benfica against Zenit St Petersburg in 2012, and the striker went on to make three appearances for his country as they reached the semi-finals at Euro 2012.

JOSH MURPHY   **11** MIDFIELDER

NATIONALITY: English   **DOB:** 24/02/1995

DID YOU KNOW: Josh's baptism into senior football was spectacular. He came off the bench against Watford in the League Cup and fired in a stunning strike that inspired City's comeback from 2-0 down to eventually triumph 3-2.

CAMERON JEROME   **10** FORWARD

NATIONALITY: English   **DOB:** 14/08/1986

DID YOU KNOW: Cameron is now in his fourth season at Carrow Road and among his highlights are scoring the Wembley opener in the Play-Off Final victory over Middlesbrough and netting Premier League away goals at Manchester City and Manchester United.

PAUL JONES **13** GOALKEEPER

NATIONALITY: Welsh **DOB:** 17/10/1990

DID YOU KNOW: While with Exeter, Paul became the first goalkeeper to save a penalty at the new Wembley Stadium during the 2006-07 Conference Play-Off Final and although Exeter missed out on promotion, Jones kept a clean sheet in the following season's Play-Off Final to help take them into the Football League.

MARLEY WATKINS **12** FORWARD

NATIONALITY: Welsh **DOB:** 17/10/1990

DID YOU KNOW: Marley scored ten times in the second tier for Barnsley last season before the versatile attacker made the move to Carrow Road in the summer.

WES HOOLAHAN **14** MIDFIELDER

NATIONALITY: Irish **DOB:** 20/05/1982

DID YOU KNOW: Wes signed from Blackpool in the summer of 2008, and last season he picked up the Player of the Season award in the year that he surpassed 300 matches for the Canaries.

TIMM KLOSE
15
DEFENDER

NATIONALITY: Swiss   **DOB:** 09/05/1988

DID YOU KNOW: The Swiss international defender's senior career began in his homeland with FC Basel's U21s, before his impressive displays for FC Thun earned him a move to Wolfsburg. Timm helped the Wolves win the German Cup and German Super Cup ahead of his move to England.

MATT JARVIS
16
MIDFIELDER

NATIONALITY: English   **DOB:** 22/05/1986

DID YOU KNOW: Matt has one cap for England, featuring for the Three Lions in a 2011 friendly against Ghana at Wembley Stadium. After moving from West Ham in January 2016, Matt missed all of last season with a knee injury.

YANIC WILDSCHUT
17
MIDFIELDER

NATIONALITY: Dutch   **DOB:** 01/11/1991

DID YOU KNOW: The Netherlands U21 was born in Amsterdam and played for a number of youth sides before joining Ajax's Academy. He arrived at City at the start of 2017 after spells with Middlesbrough and Wigan.

MARCO STIEPERMANN

18
MIDFIELDER

NATIONALITY: German   **DOB:** 09/02/1991

DID YOU KNOW: Marco made his professional debut for Borussia Dortmund in the Bundesliga in December 2009 and has represented Germany from U15 to U20 level. He joined City on a three-year deal in the summer.

TOM TRYBULL

19
MIDFIELDER

NATIONALITY: German   **DOB:** 09/03/1993

DID YOU KNOW: After joining the Canaries in August 2017, Tom scored his first goal for the club on his debut, during the EFL Cup 4-1 home win over Charlton Athletic.

ALEX PRITCHARD

21
MIDFIELDER

NATIONALITY: English   **DOB:** 03/05/1993

DID YOU KNOW: Alex is a graduate of the Spurs Academy, and while on loan at Championship side Brentford, he netted 12 times in 47 games which saw him named in the division's Team of the Year.

JAMES MADDISON 23
MIDFIELDER

NATIONALITY: English **DOB:** 23/11/1996

DID YOU KNOW: After James made his Norwich debut in August 2016, he moved on a five-month loan to Scottish Premiership side Aberdeen and while at Pittodrie, he played 17 games and made the headlines by scoring a last-minute free-kick to beat Rangers.

BEN GODFREY 22
DEFENDER

NATIONALITY: English **DOB:** 15/01/1998

DID YOU KNOW: Ben signed from York City in January 2016 on his 18th birthday. Later the same year, he came off the bench to score on his debut in the 6-1 thrashing of Coventry City in the EFL Cup.

HARRY TOFFOLO 24
DEFENDER

NATIONALITY: English **DOB:** 19/08/1995

DID YOU KNOW: Norwich City Academy graduate, Harry, was one of several players to star in the Club's famous FA Youth Cup success of 2012-13. At the start of 2017-18 he went out on loan to Doncaster Rovers.

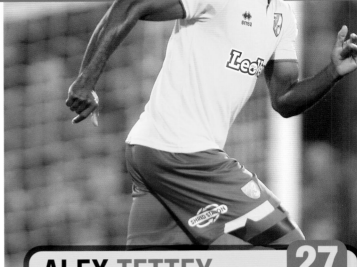

ALEX TETTEY
27 MIDFIELDER

NATIONALITY: Norwegian **DOB:** 04/04/1986

DID YOU KNOW: The Norwegian international was born in the Ghanaian capital of Accra, but moved to Norway as a youngster, and spent six seasons at Rosenborg from 2003-09. Alex has been at Norwich since 2012 and has made over 150 appearances for the club.

JAMAL LEWIS
26 DEFENDER

NATIONALITY: English **DOB:** 25/01/1998

DID YOU KNOW: Jamal is an exciting prospect and his impressive pre-season displays were rewarded with a new Canaries' contract, keeping him at Carrow Road until at least 2021.

MARCEL FRANKE
28 DEFENDER

NATIONALITY: German **DOB:** 05/04/1993

DID YOU KNOW: The towering defender is a product of Dynamo Dresden's youth system and arrived in Norwich in July 2017 on a three-year deal.

REMI MATTHEWS **29** GOALKEEPER

NATIONALITY: English   **DOB:** 10/02/1994

DID YOU KNOW: Remi, a product of Norwich's Academy, spent 2016-17 on loan to Hamilton Academical. A shoulder injury kept him out for four months, but he made a dramatic return, saving three penalties in a 3-0 shoot-out win over Dunfermline in the Scottish Cup.

MICHAEL McGOVERN **33** GOALKEEPER

NATIONALITY: Irish   **DOB:** 12/07/1984

DID YOU KNOW: Michael's great displays between the sticks have seen him become a regular for Northern Ireland, starring at Euro 2016 before making the move to Carrow Road in July 2016.

GRANT HANLEY **31** DEFENDER

NATIONALITY: Scottish   **DOB:** 20/11/1991

DID YOU KNOW: After six seasons and 200 appearances for Blackburn Rovers and one successful campaign with Newcastle United, Scottish international Grant made the move south to Carrow Road.

LOUIS THOMPSON **34** MIDFIELDER

NATIONALITY: Welsh   **DOB:** 19/12/1994

DID YOU KNOW: The young Welsh U21 international midfielder, who was signed from Swindon Town in 2014 before being loaned back to the League One club, has committed his future to the Canaries until at least 2019.

The success of any team is often built on a solid and reliable defence and the mid-80s pairing of Steve Bruce and Dave Watson at the heart of City's back four is widely recognised as one of the club's finest-ever central-defensive partnerships.

DOUBLE

Both Steve Bruce and Dave Watson were recruited under the shrewd management of Ken Brown. After forging their successful partnership at Carrow Road as Norwich tasted Milk Cup Wembley glory in 1985 and then sealed an immediate return to the top flight as Second Division Champions in 1986, both players unsurprisingly went on to enjoy highly-successful careers at the very pinnacle of the English game with Manchester United (Bruce) and Everton (Watson).

Watson was the first to arrive at Carrow Road. After finding first-team opportunities impossible to come by at Liverpool, the 19-year-old joined the Canaries in 1980 for an initial fee of £50,000 which doubled to £100,000 after 25 first-team games.

Despite suffering relegation to the Second Division in his first season, Watson played 38 league games in the following 1981-82 campaign and won the first of his two promotions while at Carrow Road.

A brave and strong defender with a great ability to read the game, Watson was named City captain midway through the 1982-83 season and ended the campaign as the club's player of the season.

His superb club form led to his first international cap as England defeated Brazil at the Maracana in 1984. It was also the summer that manager Brown secured the services of a new central defensive partner for Watson in the shape of Gillingham defender Steve Bruce for a fee of £135,000.

BRUCE

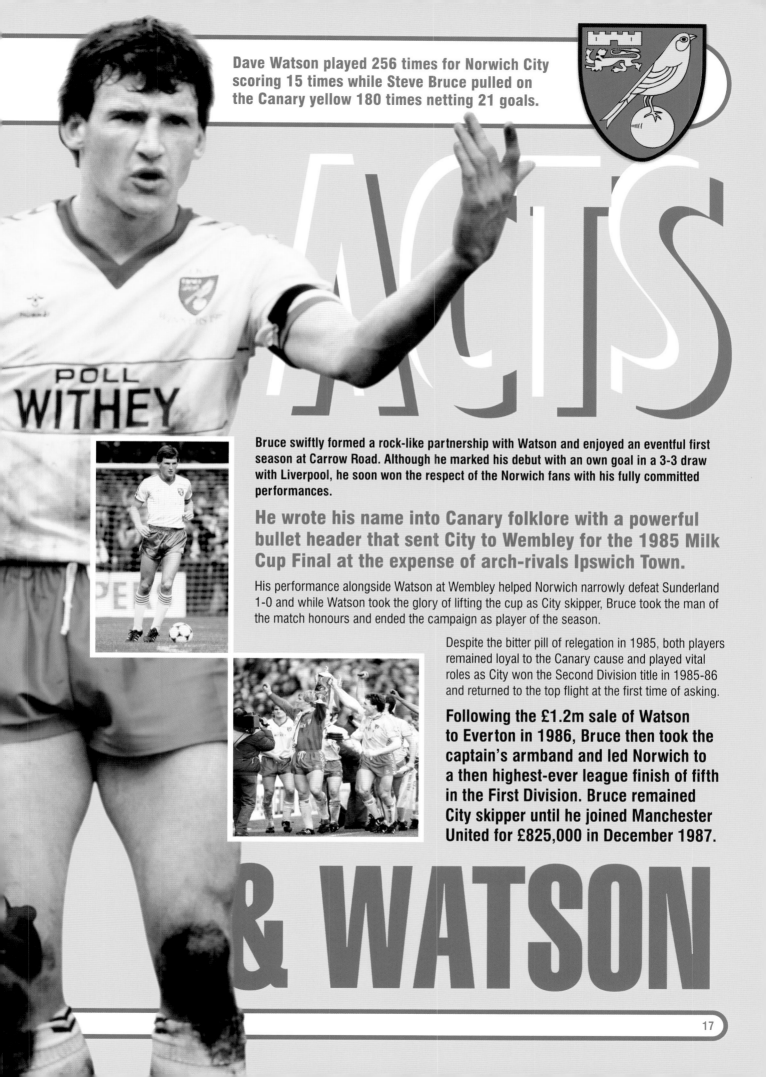

Dave Watson played 256 times for Norwich City scoring 15 times while Steve Bruce pulled on the Canary yellow 180 times netting 21 goals.

FACTS

Bruce swiftly formed a rock-like partnership with Watson and enjoyed an eventful first season at Carrow Road. Although he marked his debut with an own goal in a 3-3 draw with Liverpool, he soon won the respect of the Norwich fans with his fully committed performances.

He wrote his name into Canary folklore with a powerful bullet header that sent City to Wembley for the 1985 Milk Cup Final at the expense of arch-rivals Ipswich Town.

His performance alongside Watson at Wembley helped Norwich narrowly defeat Sunderland 1-0 and while Watson took the glory of lifting the cup as City skipper, Bruce took the man of the match honours and ended the campaign as player of the season.

Despite the bitter pill of relegation in 1985, both players remained loyal to the Canary cause and played vital roles as City won the Second Division title in 1985-86 and returned to the top flight at the first time of asking.

Following the £1.2m sale of Watson to Everton in 1986, Bruce then took the captain's armband and led Norwich to a then highest-ever league finish of fifth in the First Division. Bruce remained City skipper until he joined Manchester United for £825,000 in December 1987.

& WATSON

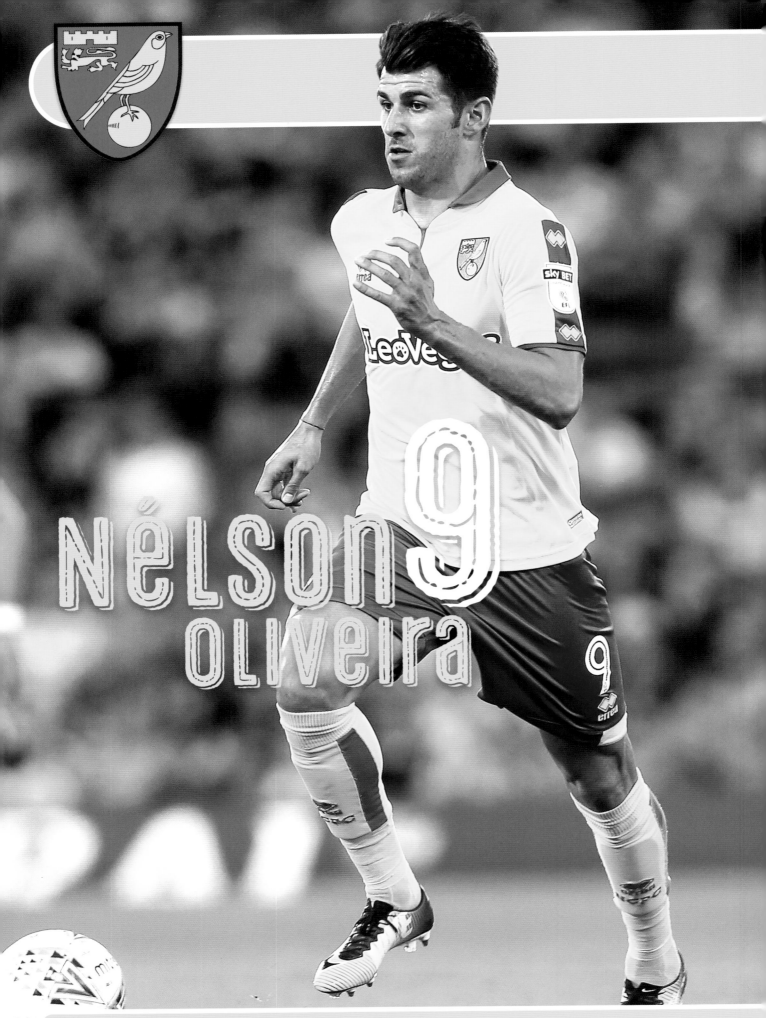

NÉLSON OLIVEIRA 9

1. LOAN RANGER.

Darren Huckerby joined Norwich City on a three-month loan deal from Manchester City in September 2003. His arrival sparked a major up-turn in City's results and thrust the club into the promotion picture. Huckerby produced some truly memorable performances during his loan spell and his pace often had the Carrow Road faithful up and off their seats. The final game of his loan was an emotional one as he turned in an outstanding performance as City beat Cardiff 4-1. Despite briefly returning to Manchester City, the loan became permanent on Boxing Day 2003.

2. GOING UP, UP, UP!

With Huckerby's services secured on a permanent basis, there was simply no stopping the Canaries as their star man propelled them to the Premier League. With undoubtedly the league's best player on their books, Norwich were unstoppable and took a giant step to securing promotion when Huckerby opened the scoring with a great solo effort in a 2-0 victory over promotion-rivals Wigan Athletic at Carrow Road on Good Friday 2004.

3. OFF TO A FLYER.

Back in the top flight after winning promotion as Nationwide First Division champions, City kicked off their Barclays Premiership campaign with an opening day fixture at home to Crystal Palace. Fittingly, it was Huckerby, the player who did so much to inspire promotion, who took the mantle of scoring the Canaries' first goal of the 2004-05 campaign - he picked up the ball in the right-hand channel before bursting into the box and driving a blistering shot past Julian Speroni in front of a delighted Carrow Road crowd.

4. DERBY DELIGHT.

There's no better way for a Norwich player to endear himself to the club's supporters than to score a winning goal against arch-rivals Ipswich Town - particularly on enemy territory. And Huckerby did just that to secure all three points and local pride when City won 1-0 at Portman Road in September 2005. Despite starting the game on the bench, Huckerby replaced Dean Marney and netted the game's only goal to be the hero of the hour once again.

5. GOAL OF THE SEASON.

Huckerby netted many great goals for the Canaries, but for sheer individual brilliance, it would have to be City's goal of the season against Birmingham City in 2006-07 that would be viewed as his finest. All of the 23,504 crowd that were inside Carrow Road on Tuesday 13 March 2007 were certainly fortunate to have been able to say 'I was there' as Huckerby single-handedly took on the Birmingham defence before netting the only goal of the game to secure three points for Peter Grant's Norwich side.

6. PLAYER OF THE SEASON DOUBLE.

Often the star performer during his five years at Carrow Road, Huckerby twice saw his name engraved on to the famous Barry Butler Memorial Trophy after he was voted by the supporters as the club's player of the season in both 2004-05 and again in 2006-07. He is one of only seven players to have won the award on more than one occasion.

DARREN'S SIX STEPS TO STARDOM

CHAMPIONSHIP KEY PLAYERS

KEIREN WESTWOOD
SHEFFIELD WEDNESDAY

Keiren's excellent displays between the sticks have been rewarded with over 20 international caps for the Republic of Ireland. The shot-stopper has made over 130 appearances each for Sheffield Wednesday, Coventry City and Carlisle United as well as being honoured with the Player of the Year award at each club!

ALEX SMITHIES
QPR

Now 27, former England U19 international Alex, was at one time rated as one of the country's hottest young goalkeepers after breaking into Huddersfield's first eleven when just 17. Despite a lot of interest, he stayed with the West Yorkshire side, playing 274 games for the Terriers until his 2015 move to the capital.

ADAM DAVIES
BARNSLEY

Although Adam was born in Germany, the 25-year-old comes from a Welsh family and although he's yet to debut, he has been a part of several Wales squads. After starting his career at Everton followed by a spell with Sheffield Wednesday, Davies is now a real safe pair of hands for the Tykes with over 100 appearances behind him.

goalkeepers

The value of a great goalkeeper just can't be underestimated. We've selected six top stoppers who will look to shine over the coming months.

FELIX WIEDWALD
LEEDS UNITED

After making the move to Yorkshire from Werder Bremen in the summer, former Germany U20 international Felix really caught the eye and did so well that he was chosen ahead of Leeds United's ex-England 'keeper Rob Green. The imposing 6ft 3ins goalie has also played in Germany with MSV Duisburg and Eintracht Frankfurt.

SCOTT CARSON
DERBY COUNTY

The former England goalkeeper is still one of the best 'keepers around. Scott commands his penalty area and has a real presence on the pitch. After starting out with a handful of appearances for both Leeds United and Liverpool, Carson has now played over 400 career games both in England and Turkey.

VITO MANNONE
READING

Vito came to England from Atalanta and continued his career at Arsenal. Following loan spells with Barnsley and Hull City, he went north to Sunderland where he was the hero of the Black Cats' run to the 2014 League Cup Final, starring in their semi-final shoot-out win against Manchester United at Old Trafford. Player of the Year at the Stadium of Light that year, Mannone moved to the Madejski Stadium last summer.

MICHAEL DAWSON
HULL CITY

Former England and Spurs centre-back, Michael made his name with Nottingham Forest before moving to the capital in 2005. The commanding defender has been voted Player of the Year with both Tottenham and the Tigers as well as winning the League Cup with Spurs a decade ago. The City skipper's consistant displays have seen him selected for the PFA Team of the Year at both ends of his career, in 2003 and 2016.

JOHN TERRY
ASTON VILLA

John is a modern-day legend. After over 700 appearances for Chelsea, and 78 for England, Terry had plenty of choices after leaving Stamford Bridge, but was convinced of Aston Villa's attractions by Steve Bruce, once a top-class centre-back himself. He has won everything going with Chelsea and has more individual awards than one trophy cabinet can hold.

RYAN SESSEGNON
FULHAM

Probably the best young player in the Championship, London-born Sessegnon is the cousin of the former Sunderland and WBA, Benin international Stephane Sessegnon. Ryan debuted for Fulham in August 2016 when he was only 16. Despite playing at left-back, he was joint top scorer at the 2017 European U19 tournament won with England.

defenders

Protecting a lead, battling for that all important clean sheet and trying to help support their attack-minded teammates - here are six top quality Championship defenders to look out for.

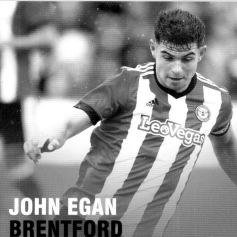

SOULEYMANE BAMBA
CARDIFF CITY

Experienced Ivory Coast international centre-back Souleymane was born in France and began his playing career with Paris Saint-Germain before a move to Dunfermline. After plying his trade in Scotland, England, Turkey and Italy, Bamba made Wales the sixth country he has called home when he signed for Neil Warnock's Bluebirds.

JOHN EGAN
BRENTFORD

The Republic of Ireland international centre-back has the happy knack of chipping in with his share of goals. He is a proper centre-back, a leader with a real hunger to keep the ball out of the net. John's dad was a famous Gaelic footballer while his mother has a League of Ireland winners medal with Cork Rangers, so it's no surprise he is a talented lad destined for the top.

NATHAN BAKER
BRISTOL CITY

After 13 years and over 100 games for Aston Villa, former England U21 international left-footed centre-back Nathan Baker signed for the Robins last summer after spending the previous season on loan at Ashton Gate. Brave and committed, Villa's loss is certainly Bristol's gain.

CHEIKH NDOYE
BIRMINGHAM CITY

A commanding 6ft 3ins powerhouse in the centre of midfield, Senegal international Cheikh moved to St. Andrew's in 2017 from French club Angers who he skippered in last season's Coupe de France final, narrowly losing 1-0 to all conquering Paris Saint-Germain. He previously played for Creteil with whom he won the Championnat National (the third division of the French football) in 2013.

AIDEN McGEADY
SUNDERLAND

With almost 100 caps for the Republic of Ireland, Aiden is one of the most magical wingers in the championship. In 2010 he commanded a fee of almost £10m when joining Spartak Moscow from Celtic with whom he had won seven trophies. He arrived at the Stadium of Light from Everton after playing for Black Cats boss Simon Grayson last season on loan to Preston.

DANIEL JOHNSON
PRESTON NORTH END

Originally from Kingston, Jamaica, Daniel progressed through the Aston Villa academy and went on a trio of loans before Preston signed him in January 2015. Eight goals from midfield from 23 games that season helped power Preston to promotion.

midfielders

The Championship is packed with top-class midfield performers - we've chosen six midfield maestros who could well be real star turns for their respective clubs this season.

NATHAN THOMAS
SHEFFIELD UNITED

A talented and exciting winger, Nathan made the jump from, just relegated from League Two Hartlepool, to just promoted from League One Sheffield United and got off to a flying start with a debut goal in a League Cup win over Walsall. He likes to score the spectacular, finding the back of the net nine times for struggling Hartlepool last season and it's only a matter of time until Nathan is a fans' favourite at Bramall Lane.

JEM KARACAN
BOLTON WANDERERS

Jem is at his best when he's hassling and disrupting the opposition's midfield with his typically high-energy performance. London -born to an English mother and Turkish father, Jem has played for Turkey at junior levels and been in full international squads, but has yet to make his full international debut. He has played club football in Turkey as well as England and after starting over 150 games for Reading, he joined Bolton from Galatasary in 2017.

RUBEN NEVES
WOLVES

Wanderers' Portuguese international record-signing midfielder from Porto cost a reported £15.8m in 2017. Neves is just 20, but reads the game like a seasoned professional and seems destined for the top. Wolves hope this natural leader will guide them to the Premier League. Ruben is also the youngest player to captain a team in the Champions League, Porto at the age of 18.

CHAMPIONSHIP KEY PLAYERS

MARVIN SORDELL
BURTON ALBION

Still only 26, Marvin seems to have been around for a long time. He represented Great Britain at the 2012 London Olympics and has also played for England at U21 level. He made his name with Watford and once commanded a big money move into the Premier League with Bolton. He is a consistent and versatile performer who likes to shoot from distance.

STEVE MORISON
MILLWALL

33-year-old Steve is a Lions legend. He is now in his third spell with the club and is the reigning Millwall Player of the Year. The towering striker, and former Canary, has scored over 230 goals in a career that started in 2001 with Northampton Town and has seen him play for England at 'C' level (non-league), before becoming a full international with Wales.

DARYL MURPHY
NOTTINGHAM FOREST

The Republic of Ireland international was the Championship's top scorer in 2014-15 with Ipswich Town when the targetman's power and pace also earned him the Tractor Boys' Player of the Year award. He won Premier League promotion with Newcastle United last season and Sunderland in 2007 and also had a spell with Celtic in the SPL at the start of the decade.

forwards

Goals win games and when it comes to finding the back of the net at Championship level they don't come much sharper than these six great goal getters.

BRITT ASSOMBALONGA
MIDDLESBROUGH

Britt is arguably, considered the best striker outside the Premier League. He is a proven goalscorer in the Championship, scoring 30 goals in 47 league starts for Forest. The Teessiders invested £15m to bring in the son of a former Zaire international and if he stays injury-free, could fire the Boro back into the Premier League.

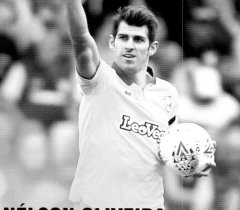

NÉLSON OLIVEIRA
NORWICH CITY

The Portugal international is a threatening striker, quick off the mark with first-class technique and neat footwork. Nélson, who started with Benfica, had six loans with clubs in Portugal, France, England and Wales, before committing his future to the Carrow Road club in 2016. He scored 15 times in 31 games in his first season as a Canary and commenced the current campaign with three goals in his first three matches.

MARTYN WAGHORN
IPSWICH TOWN

The former England U21 international returned to the English league last summer after two years in Scotland with Rangers where he won a Player of the Year award to go with the Young Player of the Year trophy he won with Leicester. Martyn has the ability to play anywhere across the front four and his good scoring record continued this season with four goals in his first three Championship games.

WHAT BALL?

There are too many footballs! Can you work out which is the real ball in each photo.

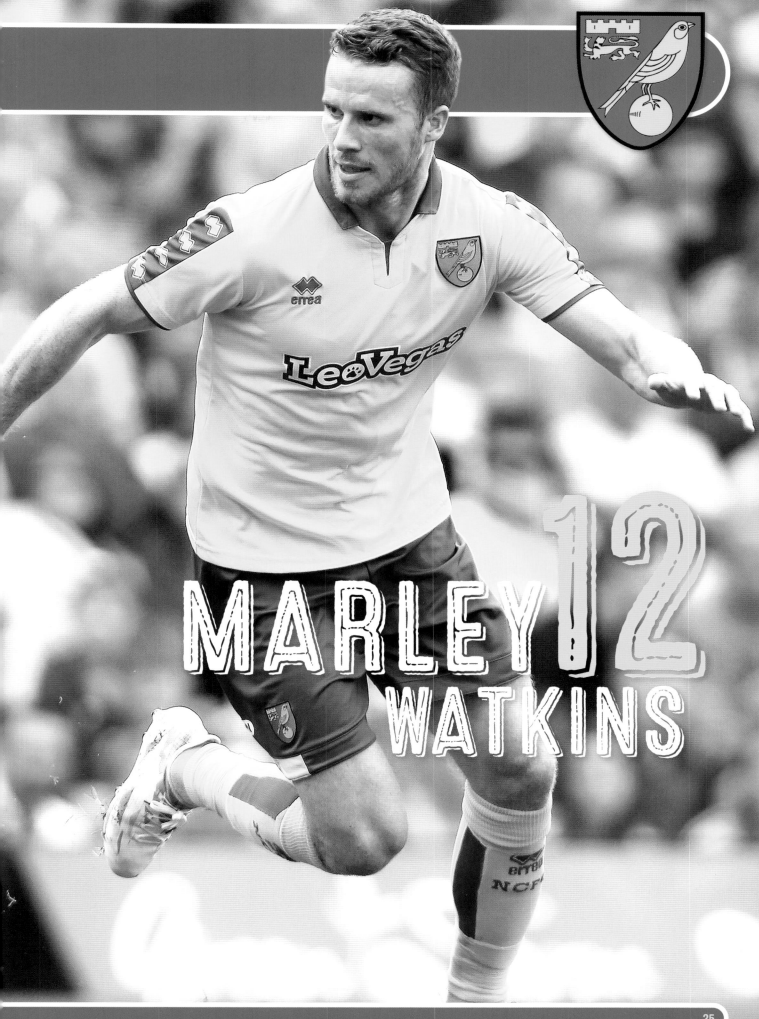

MARLEY **12**
WATKINS

1

4

5

3

2

6

26

WHO ARE YA?

7 8 9 10

TRAINING TO WIN

Preparation is certainly a key ingredient to success in professional football. All the work that takes place at the club's busy Colney training centre is geared to ensuring that Daniel Farke's men are fully equipped for the challenges that lie ahead.

The days of Ron Saunders putting his City players through their paces in pre-season on Mousehold Heath in the 1970s are certainly a thing of the past. The modern-day player will not only be given the best of surfaces to practice on, but also given the very best advice and guidance in terms of their fitness, diet, rest and mental approach to performing at their maximum.

A typical day at Colney will begin at 9am with a series of physical tests, being weighed and taking part in a number of aerobic exercises before blood levels and heart rates are measured.

Diet is vital to any players' wellbeing and performance levels, hence a suitable breakfast is provided at Colney before players head to the gymnasium to do their own personal work-outs.

Prior to taking to the training pitches, players will be provided with a GPS tracking system and heart rate analysis monitors ensuring that all they do can be measured, monitored and reviewed.

A period of pre-activation activities then take place before further physical conditioning begins out on the grass. The manager and coaches will then get down to working on various drills, set-piece situations and practice matches in the day's main session.

An ice bath and suitable warm-down programme will then take place before lunch and a return to the gym where a strength, power and injury presentation session takes place and feedback on the day's activity will be provided by the sports science department.

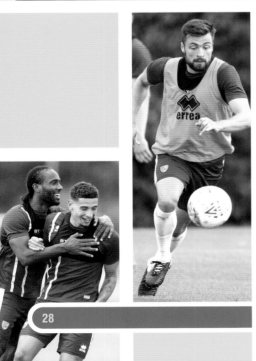

IVO 2
PINTO

FOOTBALL 50

Here is a list of 50 footie words. All but one are hidden in the grid, can you work out which is missing?

```
S U B S T I T U T E I S R E D L E I F D I M
M A A Z P L E A O S U J J Y O Y T N D T R K O
A Q E X T R A T I M E R L C K J A U D I M E
N B L C A C A D E M Y K F Y U K O B C B N P
O N I E S A J W R T P E X R T G D K H B P B
F R F J A P H I A E M R Y C U C O C A L T L
T H I W Y T D B K W S T O D Y F B R L I E I
H D N E P A R X J B I S C M F A U O L N E T
E D A Z L I N E S M A N I T O F D G E G H R
M B L D S N W A E C Q I U N A T P U N Q S A
A I W Y H C O R N E R F L A G O I M G Z N N
T E H E A D E R V L H Y S R I R C O E R A S
C B I M J E E L U R E D I S F F O K N V E F
H G S G Q F P R N U A L K L G I H O B M L E
F R T U F E L N B T F E R E G A N A M A C R
M E L K E N G F B Y D H T D A F V G O H J W
Y K E F C D R P O C M F H L H J W G A B H I
S I O W O E K S P U I A O A V S N F D M I N
A R W M N R Q N R P L H T U O E M S R T J D
O T K C I K E E R F Y T D C D J Y B A G T O
G S O V T C A D T B R X N L H S F A C U P W
K A M P Q E T I C I E F O M R N G E W B S U
C I A M S K M R C A S G C G O U K O O C E M
I Y E J A E R K D I R F H S R E Y A L P V C
K C T E P D R G B F K D A E U G A E L E R S
R E T L T N W T J N G E Q U A L I S E R E H
O Y S P A I A W N G S R C V S F G L Y F S R
S S R N T N H L H E L S U N U T M E G U E N
S K I J S J E V R L C W A S P O L S O F R J
I K F P F H M P L K U F E H E L A O E T I M
C R O S S B A R S C T T M R O J I R W T Q N
S O I R M E X I C A N W A V E P E O L D K P
G A S U N N A E R T U B R E P E E K L A O G
```

ACADEMY
CAPTAIN
CENTRE SPOT
CHALLENGE
CLEAN SHEET
CORNER FLAG
CROSSBAR
DEFENDER
DERBY MATCH
DRESSING ROOM
DRIBBLING
DUGOUT
EQUALISER
EXTRA TIME
FA CUP
FANS
FINAL WHISTLE
FIRST TEAM
FIXTURE
FOUL
FREE KICK
GOALKEEPER
GOLDEN GOAL
HALF TIME
HAT-TRICK
HEADER
INJURY TIME
KICK-OFF
LEAGUE
LINESMAN
MANAGER
MAN OF THE MATCH
MEXICAN WAVE
MIDFIELDER
NUTMEG
OFFSIDE RULE
PENALTY
PLAYERS
PRE-SEASON
PROMOTION
RED CARD
REFEREE
RESERVES
SCISSOR KICK
STRIKER
SUBSTITUTE
TACKLE
TRANSFER WINDOW
VOLLEY
YELLOW CARD

2017-18

BACK ROW (LEFT TO RIGHT): Lee Dunn, Dan Smith, Tom Trybull, Josh Murphy, Yanic Wildschut, Cameron Jerome, Mario Vrančić, Russell Martin, Marley Watkins, Nélson Oliveira, Ivo Pinto, Alex Tettey, Stuart Wardle, Charlie Radmore.

MIDDLE ROW (LEFT TO RIGHT): **Charles Cullen, Damien Bowyer, Dan Savage, Marco Stiepermann, Marcel Franke, Christoph Zimmermann, Paul Jones, Angus Gunn, Remi Matthews, Michael McGovern, Timm Klose, Grant Hanley, Jamal Lewis, Ed Wootten, Brenton Egglestone, Rhys Owen.**

BOTTOM ROW (LEFT TO RIGHT): **Shaun Spurdens, Steve Rigby, Wes Hoolahan, Steven Naismith, Harrison Reed, Louis Thompson, Chris Domogalla, Daniel Farke, Edmund Riemer, Christian Fluethmann, James Maddison, James Husband, Matt Jarvis, Alex Pritchard, Glyn Lewis, Chris Budd.**

WES HOOLAHAN

2017 PLAYER OF THE YEAR

If you pick your all-time Norwich XI, there is strong competition in almost all positions. Deadly strikers, a succession of pacey, tricky wingers, classy central midfielders, gnarled centre-backs, crafty full-backs, athletic goalkeepers.

One area stands alone, though. The No.10. Wes Hoolahan is like no player we have seen in a Norwich shirt. His gifts are rare in British and Irish football. It is why fans often say we may never see the like of him again - it's not a throwaway cliché, it's because his talent is unique. At his best, Wes slows the game down when he's on the ball; the match marches to his rhythm.

The No.10 role is so ideally suited to him that it's a surprise to learn he never even considered playing there until Paul Lambert took him to one side before a League One game in 2009 and suggested he would be more productive in the hole than out on the left wing. He hasn't looked back.

We've been lucky to have him, and even luckier to have had him for so long. Last season he reached 300 appearances for the Canaries, a rare feat in modern football. As Wes himself said at the time: "It's quite rare in modern football to be at a Club for that long. But it's been great. Every minute of it."

It was fitting reward that he was voted Player of the Season at the end of last season's campaign and, as he enters his tenth season for the club, there are no signs of him slowing down anytime soon.

THE BARRY BUTLER MEMORIAL TROPHY

Named in honour of the club captain who tragically lost his life in a car accident in 1966.

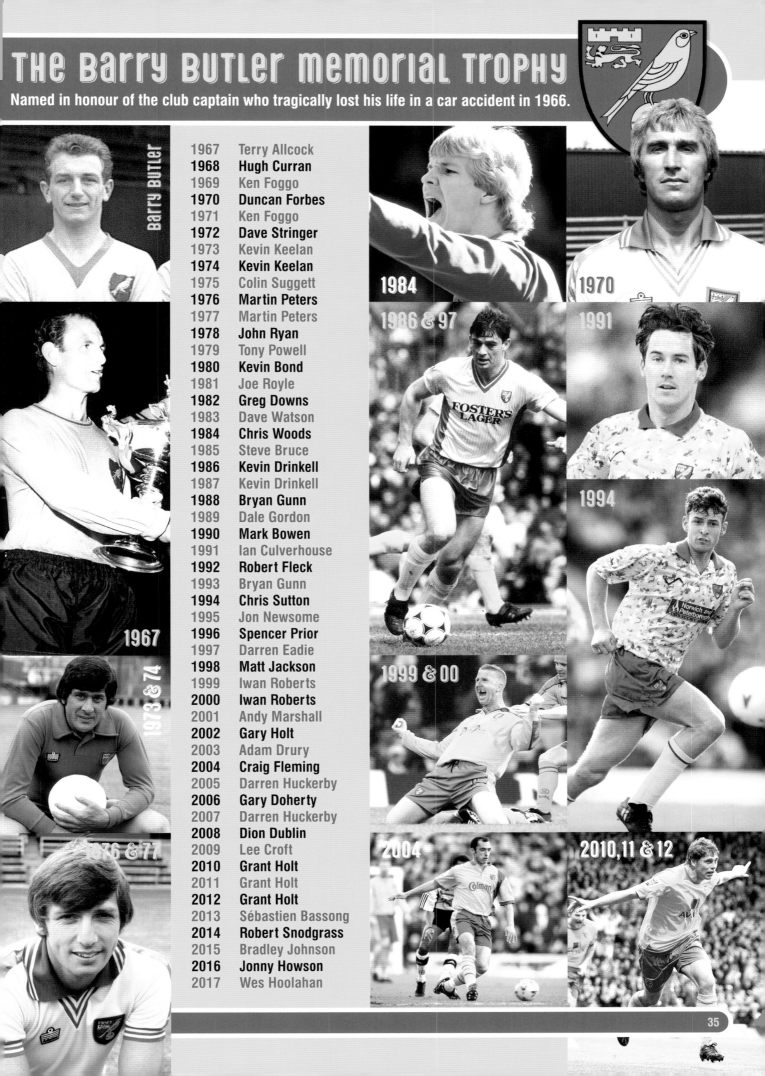

Barry Butler

Year	Winner
1967	Terry Allcock
1968	Hugh Curran
1969	Ken Foggo
1970	Duncan Forbes
1971	Ken Foggo
1972	Dave Stringer
1973	Kevin Keelan
1974	Kevin Keelan
1975	Colin Suggett
1976	Martin Peters
1977	Martin Peters
1978	John Ryan
1979	Tony Powell
1980	Kevin Bond
1981	Joe Royle
1982	Greg Downs
1983	Dave Watson
1984	Chris Woods
1985	Steve Bruce
1986	Kevin Drinkell
1987	Kevin Drinkell
1988	Bryan Gunn
1989	Dale Gordon
1990	Mark Bowen
1991	Ian Culverhouse
1992	Robert Fleck
1993	Bryan Gunn
1994	Chris Sutton
1995	Jon Newsome
1996	Spencer Prior
1997	Darren Eadie
1998	Matt Jackson
1999	Iwan Roberts
2000	Iwan Roberts
2001	Andy Marshall
2002	Gary Holt
2003	Adam Drury
2004	Craig Fleming
2005	Darren Huckerby
2006	Gary Doherty
2007	Darren Huckerby
2008	Dion Dublin
2009	Lee Croft
2010	Grant Holt
2011	Grant Holt
2012	Grant Holt
2013	Sébastien Bassong
2014	Robert Snodgrass
2015	Bradley Johnson
2016	Jonny Howson
2017	Wes Hoolahan

1984

1970

1986 & 97

1991

1994

1967

1973 & 74

1976 & 77

1999 & 00

2004

2010, 11 & 12

IN HIS TESTIMONIAL SEASON, WE TAKE A LOOK AT SIX REASONS FOR WES HOOLAHAN'S POPULARITY AT CARROW ROAD...

1. STAYING LOYAL.
Despite suffering relegation from the Championship at the end of his first season at Carrow Road, Hoolahan remained loyal to the club and played a key role in helping the Canaries win promotion the following season. His commitment to the Canary cause won him respect from supporters and he chipped in with eleven league goals as City stormed to the League One title.

2. HAT-TRICK HERO.
After winning the League One title in 2009-10, the Canaries were showing real momentum in the Championship the following season and Hoolahan played a vital part in helping City land another three points with a hat-trick in a 4-2 victory over Sheffield United at Carrow Road. Despite starting the game as a substitute during the hectic Christmas period, Hoolahan replaced Simeon Jackson with devastating effect as the Canaries ended 2010 in winning style.

3. INTO THE BIG TIME.
Having helped inspire back-to-back promotions from League One to the Premier League, Wes marked his Premier League debut with his first top-flight goal. The Irishman sparked major celebrations among the travelling masses when he slotted home to cancel out Ben Watson's opener for the Latics and ensure City picked up a point on day one.

4. PLAY-OFF SUCCESS.
Hoolahan was very much the hero of the hour as he opened the scoring the epic Play-Off semi-final second-leg victory over arch-rivals Ipswich Town in May 2015. After City were awarded a 50th minute penalty, Carrow Road held its breath as Hoolahan stepped up in front of the Barclay and held his nerve to ram the ball past Bartosz Bialkowski and spark scenes of delight among the home fans. After sealing a semi-final victory over Ipswich, Hoolahan was instrumental in helping City overcome Middlesbrough at Wembley to secure an immediate return to the Premier League.

5. EURO HERO.
Hoolahan, Robbie Brady and Martin Olsson ensured Norwich City made their mark at the 2016 European Championships in France. Hoolahan took the tournament by storm and netted his country's first goal of the competition. He then produced a man of the match performance that culminated in him setting up Brady for a historic winner against Italy to ensure his country progressed to the last 16.

6. PLAYER OF THE SEASON.
Among the current squad, Hoolahan remains the club's longest-serving player and his popularity remains sky high. With a host of memorable goals and match-winning performances down the years, it was something of a surprise that it took until his ninth season with the club to win the player of the season award. Hoolahan was finally presented with the Barry Butler memorial trophy at the end of 2016-17 campaign and added his name to a host of Canary legends.

WES'S
SIX STEPS TO STARDOM

WES 14
HOOLAHAN

THE CHAMPIONSHIP

ASTON VILLA

Which England and Chelsea legend did Aston Villa sign at the start of this season?

1 answer

Aston Villa won the European Cup in 1981. Did they beat Bayern Munich, Barcelona or Real Madrid in the final?

2 answer

Who is the former Sunderland manager who started the season as Villa manager?

3 answer

BARNSLEY

During the summer Barnsley signed Ezekiel Fryers from which Premier League London club?

5 answer

Who is Barnsley's captain?

4 answer

Who is the Tykes' manager?

6 answer

BIRMINGHAM CITY

When did Birmingham City last win the League Cup?

8 answer

Who scored Blues first league goal this season?

7 answer

City completed a record signing on transfer deadline day, summer 2017. Who was it?

9 answer

BOLTON WANDERERS

How many times have Bolton won the FA Cup?

10 answer

Bolton reached the League Cup final in 2004 but lost to which club who are also now in the Championship?

11 answer

Name the manager who led Bolton to promotion in 2017 in his first season at the club.

12 answer

BRENTFORD

Brentford are West London rivals of QPR who they knocked out of this season's Carabao Cup away from home. Did they win 3-1, 4-1 or 5-1?

13 answer

Who is Brentford's Number 9 striker this season?

14 answer

Who was the manager of Brentford from 2013 to 2015 who went on to manage Rangers and Nottingham Forest?

15 answer

BRISTOL CITY

Which Premier League team did City knock out of the Carabao Cup away from home in the second round this season?

17 answer

Who was Bristol City's Player of the Season in 2016-17?

16 answer

Which Wales international was on loan from Sunderland to Bristol City last season?

18 answer

CHALLENGE

Let's see how well you know the Canaries and their Championship rivals...

BURTON ALBION

Who was Burton's first summer signing ahead of the 2017-18 season?

20

Which former England international began the season as Burton's manager?

19

Which former Liverpool and Villa player signed for Burton at the start of the season?

21

CARDIFF CITY

Cardiff City are the Bluebirds, but what colour were their shirts between 2012 and 2015?

22

Who was the manager who inspired Cardiff to maximum points from their first five league games of this season?

23

Who was the Chile international midfielder who moved from Cardiff to Inter Milan in 2014 and stayed with the Italian giants until 2017?

24

DERBY COUNTY

Which Derby player scored the opening goal at the Stadium of Light this season?

25

In what year did Derby win the FA Cup?

26

Who is the former England international Derby re-signed for a second spell at the club at the start of this season?

27

FULHAM

Who is Fulham's No 1 this season?

29

Which Spanish side beat Fulham in the final of the 2010 Europa League?

28

Who is Fulham's No 10 and their captain this season?

30

HULL CITY

Which country did Leonid Slutsky manage before taking over at Hull?

32

What is Hull's nickname?

31

Hull reached the FA Cup final in 2014, but lost to which London club?

33

IPSWICH TOWN

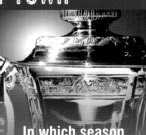

Who scored Town's first league goal this season?

34

Ipswich went from the third division to top flight champions in six years under the manager who later won the World Cup for England. Who was that?

35

In which season did the Tractor Boys win the FA Cup?

36

THE CHAMPIONSHIP

LEEDS UNITED

What is Leeds United's club anthem?

37

Between 1965 and 1974, how many times did Leeds finish in the top two of the league?

38

Who is captaining the Whites this season?

39

MIDDLESBROUGH

Which Spanish team beat Middlesbrough in the 2006 Europa League final?

41

Who did Boro sign on a season-long loan from Swansea City in July 2017?

40

Which major trophy did Boro win in 2004?

42

MILLWALL

Who did Millwall play in the 2004 FA Cup final?

44

Millwall began this season with one of their former Players of the Year as manager. Who?

43

What is Millwall's nickname?

45

NORWICH CITY

Which team did Head Coach, Daniel Farke, manage before joining City this season?

46

How many League Cup finals have Norwich played in, two, three or four?

47

Who is the Canaries No.1 this season?

48

NOTTINGHAM FOREST

Which Premier League club did Forest defeat away from home in the Carabao Cup in August 2017?

49

Forest have twice won the European Cup (now the Champions League). True or false?

50

Who is the former Brighton, Leeds and Sunderland midfielder Forest signed in August 2017?

51

PRESTON NORTH END

Who was the future Everton and Manchester United manager who won the Division Two title with Preston in 2000?

53

Who was Preston's top scorer last season?

52

Preston did it first in 1996, Wolves equalled it in 1988 and Burnley, Sheffield United and Portsmouth have done it since. What is the feat these five clubs have achieved?

54

CHALLENGE

Let's see how well you know the Canaries and their Championship rivals...

QUEENS PARK RANGERS

Which defender did Rangers pay a club record £12.5m for in 2013 only to sell him later that year?

`56`

Who is QPR's captain this season?

`55`

Which of the following managers have not managed QPR: Harry Redknapp, Mark Hughes, Martin O'Neill and Ian Holloway?

`57`

READING

Which former Manchester United defender was manager of Reading at the start of the season?

`58`

What position in the Championship did Reading finish in last season?

`59`

Who did Reading sign from Sunderland during the summer?

`60`

SHEFFIELD UNITED

Who is the Blades' No 9 striker this season?

`61`

How many points did Sheffield United earn in winning League One last season: 95, 100 or 105?

`62`

Goalkeeper Jamal Blackman is on a season long loan to Sheffield United from which Premier League London club?

`63`

SHEFFIELD WEDNESDAY

Sheffield Wednesday are one of the oldest clubs in the world. In 2017 they celebrated a major anniversary. How many years old were the club in 2017?

`65`

Who was Sheffield Wednesday's first 2017 summer signing?

`64`

Adding together Sheffield Wednesday's top flight league titles, FA Cup and League Cup wins, how many major trophies have they won: 6, 7 or 8?

`66`

SUNDERLAND

How many other current Championship clubs have Sunderland met in FA Cup finals?

`68`

Who did Sunderland sign from West Brom on August 2017 transfer deadline day?

`67`

Which two academy produced players scored their first goals for the club in August 2017?

`69`

WOLVERHAMPTON WANDERERS

Who were last season's League Cup finalists who Wolves knocked out of this season's Carabao Cup in August?

`70`

Between 1950 and 1960, how many times did Wolves finish in the top two of the top flight?

`71`

Who is the Portuguese midfielder Wolves paid almost £16m in the summer of 2017?

`72`

ANSWERS ON PAGE 62

41

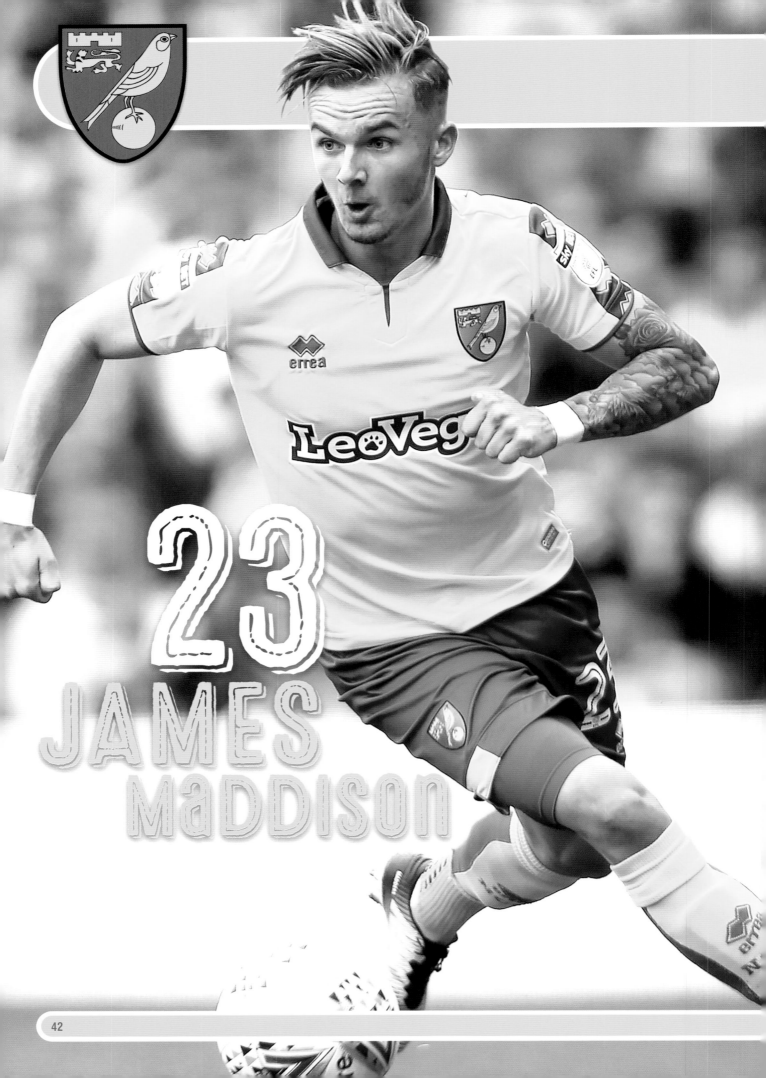

23

JAMES MADDISON

GRANT HOLT A TRUE CANARIES LEGEND

1. CAPTAINING THE CHAMPIONS.
Grant Holt enjoyed a dream first season at Carrow Road. He was swiftly handed the captain's armband by new manager Paul Lambert and proved to be an inspirational leader. He amassed a highly-impressive 30 goals in all competitions as City returned to the second tier of English football at the first time of asking by winning the League One title. Holt ended his debut-season with the club by landing the player of the season award.

2. DERBY DAY HERO.
Holt wrote his name into Norwich City folklore with a hat-trick in the East Anglian derby on 29 November 2010 as City thrashed arch-rivals Ipswich Town 4-1 at Carrow Road. Following the match, he put his boots from the game up for auction with proceeds being donated to the Special Care Baby Unit at the Norfolk and Norwich University Hospital.

3. PROMOTION TO THE PREMIER LEAGUE.
Not satisfied with leading City to promotion in 2009-10, Holt did it again as the club sealed back-to-back promotions and a return to the Premier League. Once again, Holt's goals provided the catalyst for success. The popular striker hammered home 21 league goals, including the aforementioned hat-trick against Ipswich and a second hat-trick against Scunthorpe United as City closed in on promotion.

4. SILENCING THE KOP.
Plying his trade in the top flight of English football for the first time, Holt relished proving the doubters wrong as he demonstrated that he could certainly mix it with the big boys. The Carrow Road crowd favourite scored 15 Premier League goals, including a thumping header in front of the Kop at Anfield to ensure Norwich were rewarded with a point from their trip to Merseyside. City ended their 2011-12 campaign with a comfortable 12th place finish in the Premier League.

5. PLAYER OF THE SEASON HAT-TRICK.
At the conclusion of the 2011-12 season, after City had amassed 47 points, Holt made Norwich City history. He became the first player to receive the Barry Butler Memorial Trophy as the club's player of the season on three occasions. It was a fitting honour for a player who had been a true driving force behind the club's incredible rise from League One to the Premier League in three seasons.

6. RETURNING HERO.
Despite leaving Norwich City at the end of the 2012-13 season, Holt remains a highly popular and respected figure in Norfolk. He returned to Carrow Road in December 2014 while on loan to Huddersfield Town and received a rapturous welcome from the City fans - such a response to an opposition player is unlikely to be ever seen again. Holt has since appeared twice in end of season charity matches at Carrow Road to support the club's Community Sports Foundation scheme.

GRANT'S SIX STEPS TO STARDOM

WORLD CUP

WHEN THE SEASON COMES TO AN END IN MAY, THE FOOTBALL DOESN'T STOP!

When Norwich's campaign is over and the Championship prizes are handed out, you can sit back and get ready to watch the World's international super-stars take to the pitch for the 2018 FIFA World Cup which starts on 14 June.

Just to get you in the mood, try this World Cup quiz!

1930

The first World Cup was won by the host nation Uruguay, but who did they defeat 4-2 in the Final?

1950

During England's first-ever World Cup in Brazil, they were beaten 1-0 by a team of part-timers from which country?

1966

Norwich's mascot is Captain Canary, but what was the name of the official World Cup mascot when England beat Germany 4-2 to win the World Cup?

1934

The host nation were victorious again! Italy beat Czechoslovakia 2-1, but do you know how many times the Italians have won the World Cup?

Which country scored 27 goals, the most of the tournament? Ferenc Puskás netted four of them!

1954

1970

Arguably the greatest World Cup final of all time was in 1970, when brilliant Brazil won 4-1. Who did they beat?

1938

Italy retained the trophy with a 4-2 victory over Hungary, in which European capital?

1958 & 1962

The same name went on the trophy in 1958 and 1962, the first and second of their record five wins. Who are they?

1974

The Dutch captain produced one of the World Cup's most iconic moments - a 180 degree wrong-footing turn that totally outwitted the defender. What is the move called?

QUIZ...

1978
Who was the Golden Boot winner with six goals, including two in the final?

1994

The record for most goals in a single match by one player is five, scored by Oleg Salenko as Cameroon were crushed 6-1 by which nation?

2006
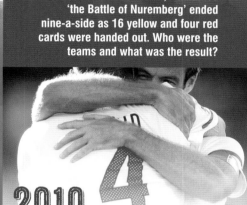
One match, nicknamed 'the Battle of Nuremberg' ended nine-a-side as 16 yellow and four red cards were handed out. Who were the teams and what was the result?

1982

Which Norwich City midfield maestro captained Northern Ireland just weeks after spearheading the Canaries promotion to the first division?

1998
Who won the Golden Ball award for the tournament's best player?

2010
Only one country remained unbeaten throughout the whole tournament. Which nation was it?

1986

Which legendary Argentinian scored twice to knock England out at the quarter-final stage 2-1?

2002

This German star scored a hat-trick in the 8-0 demolition of Saudi Arabia - the first of his record 16 goals in World Cup finals. Who is he?

2014

Which country staged the last World Cup in 2014 and who are the World Cup holders?

1990
Which Canaries striker played twice for Scotland at Italia '90?

2018
Where are the World Cup finals going to be held next summer?

ANSWERS ON PAGE 62

45

The craft and guile of Ian Crook coupled with the energy and will-to-win of Jeremy Goss provided the midfield axis that spurred Norwich City on to third place in the inaugural Premier League and an exciting UEFA Cup run in 1993-94.

DOUBLE

By his own admission, Jeremy Goss' role in the City midfield was a very straight forward one. 'Win the ball and give it to Ian Crook', was the simple instruction from manager Mike Walker.

If ever there were two players who complimented one another it was Crook and Goss. With the ball at his feet, Crook could spray the ball wherever it needed to be and his eye for a defence-splitting pass was second to none. For all his technical ability, Crook was not one for tackling, closing opponents down and tracking back to win possession.

However, in Goss, Crook had the perfect foil. In short, Goss did the running, tackling and energetic stuff for both and provided Crook with the ball to do what he did best.

Crook was one of a number of players that Norwich successfully recruited from Tottenham Hotspur in the 1980s and the £80,000 that City spent on him in June 1986 remains one of the club's best value for money signings. He went on to chalk up 418 matches and sits seventh in the Canaries' list of all-time appearance makers. His time at Carrow Road was a golden era for Norwich City as the club finished fifth, fourth and then third in the top flight and also competed in Europe for the first time.

CROOK

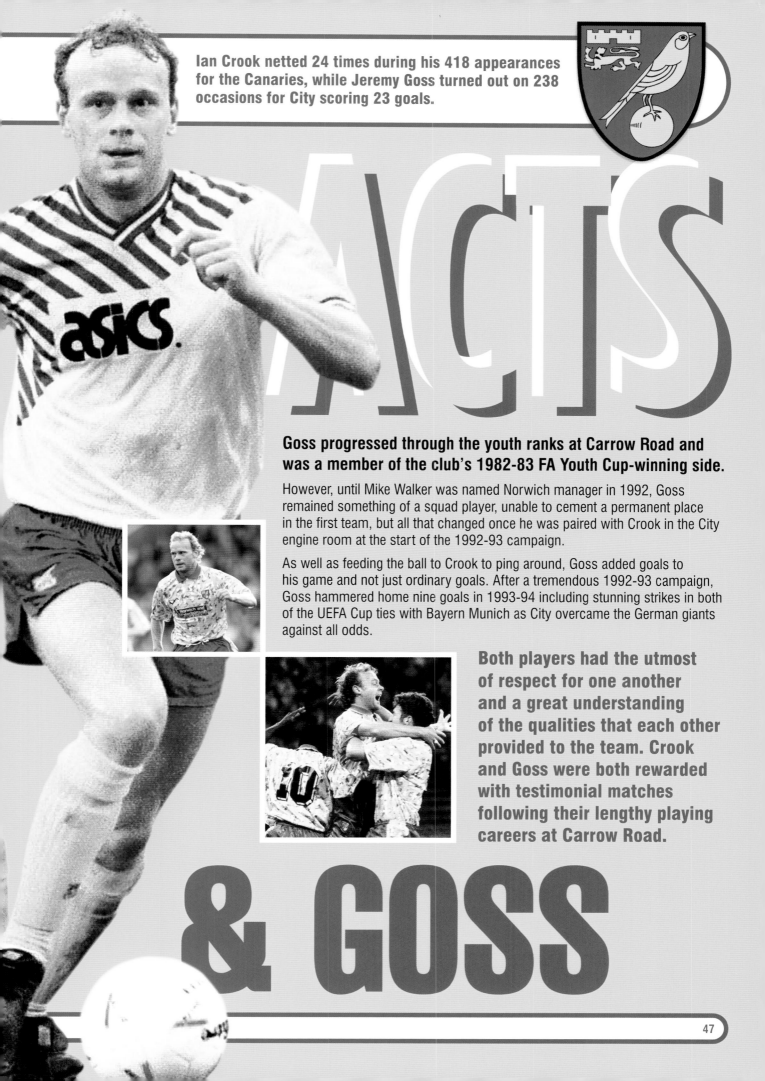

Ian Crook netted 24 times during his 418 appearances for the Canaries, while Jeremy Goss turned out on 238 occasions for City scoring 23 goals.

FACTS

Goss progressed through the youth ranks at Carrow Road and was a member of the club's 1982-83 FA Youth Cup-winning side.

However, until Mike Walker was named Norwich manager in 1992, Goss remained something of a squad player, unable to cement a permanent place in the first team, but all that changed once he was paired with Crook in the City engine room at the start of the 1992-93 campaign.

As well as feeding the ball to Crook to ping around, Goss added goals to his game and not just ordinary goals. After a tremendous 1992-93 campaign, Goss hammered home nine goals in 1993-94 including stunning strikes in both of the UEFA Cup ties with Bayern Munich as City overcame the German giants against all odds.

Both players had the utmost of respect for one another and a great understanding of the qualities that each other provided to the team. Crook and Goss were both rewarded with testimonial matches following their lengthy playing careers at Carrow Road.

& GOSS

Design their kit, add hair, be creative!

make your own FOOSBALL Team

ANGUS 1
GUNN

BOXING DAY FOOTY...

DAVID JONES

BOXING DAY 1979
Norwich City 3-3 Ipswich Town

Boxing Day was the traditional date for local derby meetings with rivals Ipswich Town and in 1979 the 23,767 inside Carrow Road were treated to a six-goal thriller.

A rare error from City goalkeeper Kevin Keelan allowed Eric Gates to open the scoring after 15 minutes. However, the Canaries roared back and led 2-1 at the break, thanks to goals from Peter Mendham and Alan Taylor.

The second half saw Town level through Arnold Muhren and then take a 3-2 lead 19 minutes from time when John Wark headed home.

Not to be denied, City grabbed a dramatic 89th minute equaliser when David Jones' powerful shot cannoned off of Keith Robson and past Town 'keeper Paul Cooper.

ALAN TAYLOR

CHRISTMAS

BOXING DAY 1985
Norwich City 3-1 Charlton

Kevin Drinkell was the toast of Carrow Road as his 13th and 14th goals of the season helped register a crucial 3-1 victory over Charlton Athletic in 1985.

This was certainly Division Two's 'Match of the Day' as table topping City hosted third placed Charlton. A tight first half ended goalless and it was the visitors who opened the scoring against the run of play through Mike Flanagan on 65 minutes.

Drinkell levelled just three minutes after the Charlton opener, but left it late to get the winner which eventually arrived after 84 minutes. John Deehan scored City's third in injury time. This proved another vital victory for Norwich who ended the season as Second Division Champions.

KEVIN DRINKELL

JOHN DEEHAN

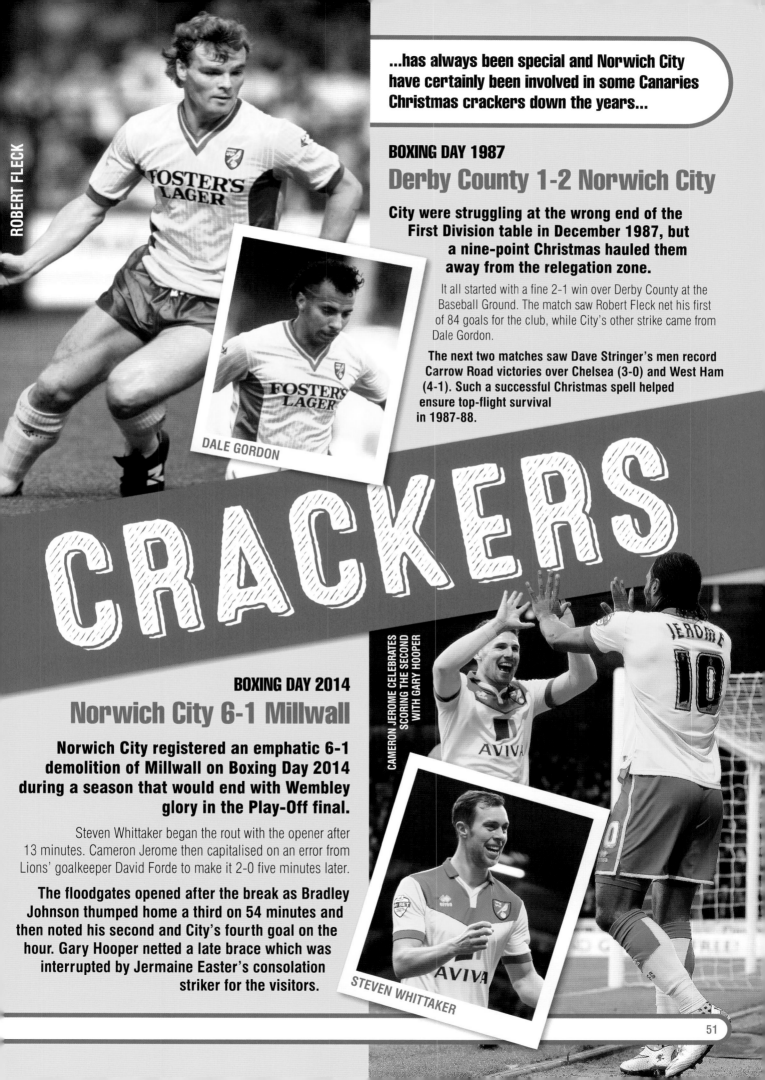

ROBERT FLECK

DALE GORDON

CAMERON JEROME CELEBRATES SCORING THE SECOND WITH GARY HOOPER

STEVEN WHITTAKER

...has always been special and Norwich City have certainly been involved in some Canaries Christmas crackers down the years...

BOXING DAY 1987
Derby County 1-2 Norwich City

City were struggling at the wrong end of the First Division table in December 1987, but a nine-point Christmas hauled them away from the relegation zone.

It all started with a fine 2-1 win over Derby County at the Baseball Ground. The match saw Robert Fleck net his first of 84 goals for the club, while City's other strike came from Dale Gordon.

The next two matches saw Dave Stringer's men record Carrow Road victories over Chelsea (3-0) and West Ham (4-1). Such a successful Christmas spell helped ensure top-flight survival in 1987-88.

CRACKERS

BOXING DAY 2014
Norwich City 6-1 Millwall

Norwich City registered an emphatic 6-1 demolition of Millwall on Boxing Day 2014 during a season that would end with Wembley glory in the Play-Off final.

Steven Whittaker began the rout with the opener after 13 minutes. Cameron Jerome then capitalised on an error from Lions' goalkeeper David Forde to make it 2-0 five minutes later.

The floodgates opened after the break as Bradley Johnson thumped home a third on 54 minutes and then noted his second and City's fourth goal on the hour. Gary Hooper netted a late brace which was interrupted by Jermaine Easter's consolation striker for the visitors.

Five Championship managers are hidden in the crowd...
Can you find them all?

FAN'TASTIC

52

YANIC 17
WILDSCHUT

DANNY MILLS

Born in the fine city of Norwich on 18 May 1977, Danny Mills began his career at Carrow Road. After playing for his home city club, the defender went on to enjoy a lengthy career in the Premier League with a number of top clubs. A full England international, the highlight of Mills' career was representing England at the 2002 World Cup finals in South Korea and Japan.

Mills progressed through the youth ranks at Norwich City before being handed his first-team debut in City's opening game of the 1995-96 season by new manager Martin O'Neill. His debut proved a highly successful one as City defeated Luton Town 3-1 at Kenilworth Road.

His tenacious tackling was used in a number of defensive roles by O'Neill, Gary Megson and Mike Walker as the local lad amassed 73 appearances for Norwich City, before sealing a move to promotion-chasing Charlton Athletic in March 1998.

After helping Charlton win promotion via the Play-Offs, Mills starred in the Premier League and sealed a £4.1 million move to Leeds United where he helped the Elland Road club progress to the Champions League semi-final before bowing out to Barcelona in the Nou Camp.

His form for Leeds won him England recognition and a career highlight would certainly have been playing in all five of England's games at the 2002 World Cup as the Three Lions progressed to the quarter-final stage under Sven-Goran Eriksson.

Mills subsequently enjoyed a League Cup triumph with Middlesbrough before joining Manchester City and ending his impressive playing career with loan spells at Hull City, Charlton and Derby County.

Since hanging up his boots, Mills has become a regular pundit and co-commentator for the BBC.

MADE IN NORWICH

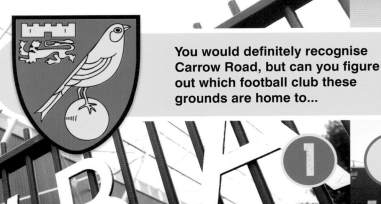

You would definitely recognise Carrow Road, but can you figure out which football club these grounds are home to...

HOME TURF

1
Team:

Ground:

Capacity:

2

Team:

Ground:

Capacity:

3

Team:

Ground:

Capacity:

4

Team:

Ground:

Capacity:

5

6

Team:

Ground:

Capacity:

7
Team:

Ground:

Capacity:

8
Team:

Ground:

Capacity:

9

Team:

Ground:

Capacity:

Team:

Ground:

Capacity:

10

Team:

Ground:

Capacity:

ANSWERS ON PAGE 62

11

...as well as their official name and capacity?!

12

Team:
Ground:
Capacity:

Team:
Ground:
Capacity:

13

Team:
Ground:
Capacity:

14

Team:
Ground:
Capacity:

15

Team:
Ground:
Capacity:

16

Team:
Ground:
Capacity:

17

Team:
Ground:
Capacity:

18

Team:
Ground:
Capacity:

19

20

Team:
Ground:
Capacity:

Team:
Ground:
Capacity:

WHAT'S GOING TO HAPPEN IN

2017-18 PREDICTIONS

CHAMPIONSHIP

OUR PREDICTION FOR ALSO PROMOTED TO THE PREMIER LEAGUE:

MIDDLESBROUGH & SUNDERLAND

YOUR PREDICTION:

OUR PREDICTION FOR CHAMPIONSHIP WINNERS:

NORWICH CITY

YOUR PREDICTION:

OUR PREDICTION FOR FA CUP WINNERS:

ARSENAL

YOUR PREDICTION:

FA CUP

PREMIER LEAGUE

OUR PREDICTION FOR PREMIER LEAGUE CHAMPIONS:

MANCHESTER UNITED

YOUR PREDICTION:

OUR PREDICTION FOR PREMIER LEAGUE RUNNERS-UP:

LIVERPOOL

YOUR PREDICTION:

OUR PREDICTION FOR PREMIER LEAGUE BOTTOM THREE:

BOURNEMOUTH, STOKE CITY & NEWCASTLE UTD

YOUR PREDICTION:

OUR PREDICTION FOR CARABAO CUP WINNERS:

MANCHESTER CITY

YOUR PREDICTION:

LEAGUE CUP

TODD CANTWELL

A great deal is expected of attacking-midfielder Todd Cantwell, as the Norwich-born teenager looks to continue his development and fulfil a dream of playing first-team football for his local club.

Schooled and raised in the mid-Norfolk market town of Dereham, Cantwell initially joined the Norwich City Academy as an under-10 and has progressed through the age groups to earn a professional contract tying him the Canary cause until the summer of 2019.

Cantwell had already grabbed the headlines even before starting his two-year scholarship with the Canaries by scoring for England under-16s in only his second outing for the Three Lions. Cantwell was on target in a 1-1 draw with Finland under-16s just 24 hours after making his debut against Denmark.

With an eye for goal and the ability to provide that defence splitting pass, Cantwell has been the creative spark for the club's under-18 and under-23 over the past three seasons.

His continual development has seen him train with the first-team squad on a number of occasions and he featured in last summer's pre-season friendly match away to Peterborough United.

Cantwell played a starring role in the under-18s run to the quarter-finals of the FA Youth Cup in 2015-16 and netted four goals as City knocked out Hull City, Sunderland and Middlesbrough before bowing out to eventual finalists Manchester City.

Last season at under-23 level, 19-year-old Cantwell played a notable part in helping the Canaries' Development Squad reach two cup semi-finals and was shortlisted for the Premier League Two, player of the season award. Cantwell was among a shortlist of eleven players, which included Liverpool's Ben Woodburn and Manchester United's Axel Tuanzebe. The award was eventually won by Swansea's Oliver McBurnie.

Whether it be bursting on to the first-team scene at Carrow Road or by gaining valuable experience on loan, 2018 could well be a breakthrough year for this promising talent.

MADE IN NORWICH

JOSH
MURPHY

ANSWERS

PAGE 24 · WHAT BALL?
A. Ball 6. B. Ball 4.

PAGE 26 · WHO ARE YA?
1. Josh Murphy. 2. James Maddison. 3. Harrison Reed.
4. Russell Martin. 5. Russell Martin. 6. Steven Naismith.
7. Mario Vrancic. 8. Marley Watkins. 9. Cameron Jerome.
10. Yanic Wildschut.

PAGE 31 · FOOTBALL 50 WORDSEARCH
The missing word is FIXTURE.

PAGE 38 · THE CHAMPIONSHIP CHALLENGE
1. John Terry. 2. Bayern Munich. 3. Steve Bruce. 4. Angus MacDonald.
5. Crystal Palace. 6. Paul Heckingbottom. 7. Craig Gardner. 8. 2011.
9. Jota. 10. Four times. 11. Middlesbrough. 12. Phil Parkinson. 13. 4-1.
14. Neal Maupay. 15. Mark Warburton. 16. Tammy Abraham.
17. Watford. 18. Adam Matthews. 19. Nigel Clough. 20. Liam Boyce.
21. Stephen Warnock. 22. Red. 23. Neil Warnock. 24. Gary Medel.
25. Bradley Johnson. 26. 1946. 27. Tom Huddlestone.
28. Atletico Madrid. 29. Marcus Bettinelli. 30. Tom Cairney.
31. The Tigers. 32. Russia. 33. Arsenal. 34. Joe Garner.
35. Sir Alf Ramsey. 36. 1977-78. 37. Marching On Together.
38. Seven. 39. Liam Cooper. 40. Connor Roberts. 41. Seville.
42. The League Cup. 43. Neil Harris. 44. Manchester United.
45. The Lions. 46. Borussia Dortmund II. 47. Four. 48. Angus Gunn.
49. Newcastle United. 50. True. 51. Liam Bridcutt. 52. Jordan Hugill.
53. David Moyes. 54. Won all four divisions of English football.
55. Nedum Onuoha. 56. Christopher Samba. 57. Martin O'Neill.
58. Jaap Stam,. 59. Third. 60. Vito Mannone. 61. Leon Clarke. 62. 100.
63. Chelsea. 64. George Boyd. 65. 150 years old, they were formed in 1867.
66. 8. 67. Callum McManaman. 68. Three: Aston Villa, Preston North
End and Leeds United. 69. George Honeyman and Lynden Gooch.
70. Southampton. 71. Six. 72. Ruben Neves.

PAGE 44 · WORLD CUP QUIZ
1930. Argentina. 1934. Four. 1938. Paris. 1950. USA. 1954. Hungary.
1958 & 1962. Brazil. 1966. World Cup Willie. 1970. Italy.
1974. The Cruyff turn, after legendary Dutch footballer Johan Cruyff.
1978. Mario Kempes. 1982. Martin O'Neill. 1986. Diego Maradona.
1990. Robert Fleck. 1994. Russia. 1998. Ronaldo.
2002. Miroslav Klose. 2006. Portugal 1-0 Netherlands.
2010. New Zealand. They drew all three of the games.
2014. Hosts: Brazil. Winners: Germany. 2018. Russia.

PAGE 52 · FAN'TASTIC

PAGE 56 · HOME TURF
1. West Bromwich Albion, The Hawthorns, 26,852.
2. Burnley, Turf Moor, 21,800.
3. Everton, Goodison Park, 39,572.
4. Arsenal, Emirates Stadium, 60,432.
5. Manchester United, Old Trafford, 75,643.
6. Aston Villa, Villa Park, 42,682.
7. Queens Park Rangers, Loftus Road, 18,439.
8. Sunderland, Stadium of Light, 49,000.
9. Ipswich Town, Portman Road, 30,311.
10. Nottingham Forest, City Ground, 30,445.
11. West Ham United, London Stadium, 57,000.
12. Fulham, Craven Cottage, 25,700.
13. Leicester City, King Power Stadium, 32,312.
14. Southampton, St Mary's Stadium, 32,505.
15. Stoke City, bet365 Stadium, 27,902.
16. Derby County, Pride Park Stadium, 33,597.
17. Wolverhampton Wanderers, Molineux Stadium, 31,700.
18. Millwall, The Den, 20,146.
19. Chelsea, Stamford Bridge, 41,663.
20. Birmingham City, St Andrew's Stadium, 29,409.

Five Championship managers are hidden in the crowd...
Can you find them all?
☐ Garry Monk ☐ Jaap Stam ☐ Neil Warnock ☐ Steve Bruce ☐ Mick McCarthy

FAN'TASTIC

ANSWERS ON PAGE 62